DOSTOEVSKY AS REFORMER:

The Petrashevsky Case

Edited and Translated by Liza Knapp

Ann Arbor, Michigan

Translated from the original Russian

Ardis Publishers
2901 Heatherway
Ann Arbor, Michigan 48104

Library of Congress Cataloging in Publication Data

Dostoevsky, Fyodor, 1821-1881.
Dostoevsky as reformer.

Bibliography: p.

1. Dostoevksy, Fyodor, 1821-1881—Trials, litigation,
etc.   2. Petrashevsky Group—Trials, litigation, etc.
3. Trials (Political crimes and offenses)—Russian
S.F.S.R.—Leningrad.   4. Courts—martial and courts of
inquiry—Russian S.F.S.R.—Leningrad.   I. Title.
LAW   345.47'0231   85-6041
ISBN 0-88233-994-X   344.705231

Contents

Dostoevsky as Reformer:
The Petrashevsky Case

> I have read it all; the case is important, for even if it is all a pack of lies, it is
> still criminal and intolerable in the highest degree.
>
> —Tsar Nicholas I, April 21, 1849[1]

Thus wrote Tsar Nicholas to the director of his secret police, Orlov, upon
having read a document reporting the activities of a group of men who would
gather on Friday nights at the Petersburg apartment of Mikhail Butashevich-
Petrashevsky to discuss political, social and literary issues of the day. These
gatherings had attracted the attention of the authorities largely because of the
reputation of their host. Aside from being an eccentric and flamboyant man,
Petrashevsky had become known as a champion of new Western ideas
considered subversive by the autocracy. In 1848, he had circulated a pamphlet
on land ownership which touched on the forbidden subject of serfdom.
Earlier, he had contributed anonymously to the *Pocket Dictionary of Foreign
Words*, a publication confiscated when the authorities realized that it had
been used by Petrashevsky and others to promote the doctrines of Fourier,
Saint-Simon, Owen, along with other Western socialists and "freethinkers."
The banning of this publication did not stop Petrashevsky, a civil servant who
worked as a translator in the Ministry of Foreign Affairs, from moonlighting
as a propagator of the ideas he espoused. He hosted weekly gatherings in his
house and developed a large library of forbidden books which he encouraged
his guests to peruse.

On Friday nights, Petrashevsky would welcome a coterie of his friends,
along with various other acquaintances. The group included civil servants,
military officers, unemployed members of the gentry, writers, teachers,
students, and even some merchants.[2] Commitment to liberal ideals varied.
For many, the Petrashevsky "circle" was primarily a social network. That
Dostoevsky considered the circle to be somewhat frivolous is attested by his
description of it, recorded by his doctor and close friend at the time, Stepan
Yanovsky. Dostoevsky told him: "As for me, I go to Petrashevsky's because
there I see some good people that I don't get to see at other people's houses; a

lot of people gather at his house because the atmosphere there is warm and free, besides which he always serves supper, and finally *at his house one can play the liberal and, indeed, who among us mortals doesn't enjoy playing that game, especially when he's had a glass of wine;* and Petrashevsky does serve wine, of course, it's bitter, vile stuff, but at least he serves it. And so all sorts of people show up..."[3]

Beginning in March of 1849, among those who would show up at Petrashevsky's was Antonelli, a former university student who had recently become Petrashevsky's colleague at work. Antonelli had been sent by the Ministry of Interior, with the consent of Orlov, the head of the Third Department (secret police), in whose domain such investigations ordinarily lay. The authorities suspected the gatherings at Petrashevsky's because people "would stay until three and four in the morning, not playing cards but reading, talking and arguing."[4] Antonelli's task was to find out who these people were and what they were arguing about.

In Antonelli's presence, enough liberal opinions were aired to convince the Ministry of the Interior that what went on at Petrashevsky's on Friday nights threatened the existing order in Russia. At this point, the Third Department was brought back into the case and Tsar Nicholas was issued a special report. He then gave the go-ahead for members of the Petrashevsky circle to be arrested. Over thirty men, among them Fyodor Dostoevsky, were imprisoned in the Peter and Paul Fortress. A lengthy investigation ensued, aimed at determining how far the "Petrashevtsy," as they came to be known, had gone and were willing to go in order to change the prevailing order in Russia.

> Life would here [in Russia] become insupportably dull and melancholy to the individual who should allow himself to reflect. In Russia, to converse is to conspire, to think is to revolt: thought is not merely a crime, it is a misfortune also.
>
> Man thinks only with a view of ameliorating his lot and that of his fellows, but when he can do nothing and change nothing, thought does but prey upon and evenom the mind, for lack of other employment.[5]

The Marquis de Custine, who wrote this description of the plight of the thinking man or woman in the Russia of Nicholas I, had travelled to Russia "in search of arguments against representative government" and "returned from Russia a partisan of constitutions." The political oppression which had distressed this foreign visitor tormented Russian subjects. Naturally, for them more was at stake than issues of comparative government.

Having come to power at the time of the Decembrist revolt of 1825, Nicholas felt it his supreme duty to protect the autocracy from all further encroachments of a democratic nature. His fear of political subversion approached paranoia. The situation observed by Custine in the late 'thirties got even worse as a result of the revolutionary upheavals in Western Europe in 1848. The authorities cracked down on conversation and thought in every way possible. The censorship, which had always been strict, became stricter (a fact boldly lamented by Dostoevsky in his deposition) and the conversations of private citizens, such as those which took place at Petrashevsky's, were monitored however possible.

This repression made both fear and secrecy rampant among the thinking people of Russia. Dostoevsky writes in his deposition:

> It has always grieved me to see how we are all as if instinctively fearful of something, to see how when we gather together in a crowd in some public place we eye each other mistrustfully, gloweringly, cast sidewise glances and act suspicious of people. Or else how when someone starts to talk, say, about politics, he is sure to start to speak in a whisper and with the most secretive look, even though the notion of a republic may be as far from his head as France.

Dostoevsky tries to convince the authorities that there is something unnatural and unhealthy in this unnecessarily furtive behavior.

Dostoevsky further explains to his interrogators that a man in his position could not help but think and indeed occasionally talk about social and political issues. Upon hearing the verdict against the Petrashevtsy, many of their contemporaries were especially horrified because they felt that "there but for the grace of God go I..." In his memoir, Petr Petrovich Semenov-Tian-Shansky, an acquaintance of many of those sentenced for their participation in the Petrashevsky circle, writes that he could find nothing criminal in their acts and that "those sentenced to death could hardly be distinguished in their outlook and aspirations from [other members of liberal circles in the 'forties]."[6] It seems that most of the thinking men of the day, with the notable exception of Gogol, believed that at least some of the changes discussed by the Petrashevtsy, were a moral imperative for Russia.

In his deposition, Dostoevsky suggests that the good intentions, which had brought him to trial, were the manifestation of an enlightened patriotism:

> Yes, if *seeking the better* is liberalism, *freethinking*, then, in this sense, perhaps, I am a freethinker. I am a freethinker in the very same sense in which one can call any man a freethinker who in the depths of his heart feels that he has the right to be a citizen, feels that he has the right to seek the welfare of his country, because in his heart he finds both love for his country and the knowledge that he has never in any way done it harm.

Dostoevsky's "freethinking" was aimed at the welfare of his fellow man. In this sense, there was little to distinguish it from the general process of thinking as it was understood by Custine when he wrote that "man thinks only with a view of ameliorating his lot and that of his fellows." But Dostoevsky and other "thinkers" of the time found themselves deprived of virtually all means of enacting change in the world around them.

In his literary works of the period, Dostoevsky explored the plight of the thinking subject of Tsar Nicholas. For example, in his feuilletons of 1847, he focuses on his fellow-citizens' desire for novelty and change.[7] Yet the capital city stagnated and along with it the rest of the empire. In these feuilletons, descriptions are couched in the whimsical terms befitting the genre (and obliging the censor). Nevertheless, Dostoevsky's thoughtful readers, trained to read between the lines, knew that when he repeatedly bemoans the lack of answer to the question "What's new?" he implies the need for positive change in the form of social reform.[8] Citizens want to be socially useful, to have a common cause and civic concerns, but these desires are frustrated by a social system designed to exclude such participation.

Thought, according to Custine, "prey[s] upon and evenom[s] the mind" of those who persist in thinking about their lot and that of their fellow men but find themselves unable to change it. The life of the thinking man becomes "insupportably dull and melancholy." Dostoevsky goes further in his feuilletons, explaining that the frustrated thinker becomes a furtive daydreamer. He depicts daydreaming as a city-wide epidemic, the result of social fragmentation and the lack of communal causes. Everyone has turned inward and places greater stock in fantasy than in reality. Dostoevsky suggests, parenthetically, that this deleterious habit may be "somehow beneficial to our general social order." What he means is that daydreaming, this ingrowth of thought, actually helps to ensure social stability under an autocratic regime and is to its clear advantage: dreamers will not rebel and try to change the existing order. Dreamers, like revolutionaries, are dissatisfied with reality. But the dreamers channel their energy into daydreams rather than into active attempts to improve the reality that disappoints them so. What's worse, habitual daydreaming eventually makes a person "unfit for real deeds." The tsar need not fear revolt from a nation of dreamers rendered incapable of activity of any sort, much less revolutionary acts.

Dostoevsky was a master of depicting the dreamer, a type figuring in many of his works of the period ("White Nights," "Netochka Nezvanova" and others). In real life, he and his companions were tempted to retreat into a dream world. In his deposition, Dostoevsky suggests that only two alternatives seem to exist for the thinking subject of the tsar—either to "petrify in isolation" (through debilitating daydreaming) or to participate in *kruzhki*, the "circles" or discussion groups which arose out of the need of the thinking populace to air its views.

Dostoevsky considered these "circles" to be an integral part of life in the capital. In his feuilletons of 1847, he asserts that "in our midst *circles* are what are most widespread. It is even a well-known fact that the whole of Petersburg is nothing more than an assembly of an enormous number of small circles." The feuilletonist offers an ostensible explanation of this phenomenon when he declares it to be "in a certain sense the product of our national character which still shies away from public life and is oriented toward home." On the other hand, Dostoevsky's readers knew from experience that people clung to the hearth because an opinion voiced anywhere else could result in disaster.

According to Dostoevsky, the gatherings which took place at Petrashevsky's and elsewhere were homey affairs rather than public meetings. "I was totally convinced," Dostoevsky informs his interrogators, "(and remain convinced to this very day) that what went on there was of a domestic nature, among a circle of Petrashevsky's mutual acquaintances and friends, and not of a public nature." Dostoevsky was wise to emphasize this point: the authorities took the fact that a small bell had been used to keep order during the discussions at the Petrashevsky home as proof of the organized, and hence political, nature of these gatherings. The bell was regarded as a "fearsome instrument of revolution."[9]

But it would have taken more than a bell to bring harmony to the gatherings at Petrashevsky's. "There was not even a shadow of unity and could not have been till kingdom come," Dostoevsky writes in his deposition. He uses this argument to make the group appear to be harmless. He wanted to convince his judges that it would have been "out of the question for there to have been some hidden, clandestine purpose in all that chaos." However, dissent was not peculiar to the Petrashevsky circle. In discussing the "circles" in his earlier feuilletons, Dostoevsky describes how the members inevitably fall victim to bickering and discord. Clearly, if these circles ever were to accomplish anything, they had to achieve greater unity of purpose.

To the disgust of some members and to the relief of others, no common cause and certainly no program emerged from all the discussion the Petrashevsky circle engaged in. A fervent advocate of judicial reform, Petrashevsky differed from many of his guests, including Dostoevsky, who considered the emancipation of the serfs to be the most pressing cause. But these were not the only topics discussed; the Petrashevtsy also addressed matters such as freedom of the press, governmental corruption, the role of religion, the social function of literature. Although the Petrashevtsy did not agree amongst themselves on these issues, many of them shared a liberal outlook and espoused certain socialist ideals. Their disagreement resulted from their differing opinions about if and how these ideals should be enacted in Russia.

In his testimony, Dostoevsky suggests that Petrashevsky's allegiance to Fourier and his utopian system, far from making him a threat to society, had rendered him politically ineffectual—that is, had made him the way the state wanted its subjects to be. Dostoevsky depicts Petrashevsky as a dreamy do-nothing and declares that Petrashevsky is "laughable but not harmful." But this portrayal of Petrashevsky as being harmless was not just a clever tactic, designed to minimize the potential threat Petrashevsky and his cohorts posed to the state. It happened to be close to Dostoevsky's actual opinion. Dostoevsky and others had gotten fed up with the fruitless chatter at Petrashevsky's and had sought to organize in such a way as to enact some of their ideas. Dostoevsky wanted to do more than daydream about change.

While still attending Petrashevsky's gatherings, Dostoevsky and some of his like-minded friends began to meet in the home of Durov and Palm. These gatherings were at first devoted to literature and music, with those attending contributing money to rent a piano. Soon sedition threatened to replace art as the common cause. Proposals were introduced to lithograph works that would promote new political ideas and stir up resentment about the mistreatment of the peasants and other groups. When Mikhail Dostoevsky (Fyodor's older brother) and others expressed alarm, the plan was discontinued and the circle began to disintegrate.

Another smaller, more cohesive group had also formed, under the leadership of Nikolai Speshnev, the figure involved in the Petrashevsky affair who is generally considered to have been the most committed revolutionary.[10] As Dostoevsky revealed to his friend Apollon Maikov, this group was devoted to "bringing about an upheaval in Russia." To this end, it acquired an illegal printing press which it planned to use to disseminate propaganda. This cabal threatened the regime more than the gatherings of the Petrashevsky circle which served as the primary focus of investigation. (The participants involved in the plot to print "subversive" literature did their best to keep the plot under wraps; two members, Speshnev and Filippov confessed to having acquired an illegal printing press, but they did not implicate the others and somehow managed to divert attention from this compromising evidence.)

The arrest of most of its members cut short the activity of the group. (The printing press had not yet been used.) Thus it is not known how far they would have gone in attempting to "bring about an upheaval in Russia." Papers found upon Speshnev's arrest suggest a theoretical commitment to violence, but whether or not all members were in agreement and would have promoted actual violence cannot be known.[11] Some evidence suggests that Dostoevsky at the time felt that he was in above his head. Exerting strong influence on him was Speshnev, the man whom Dostoevsky regarded as his "Mephistopheles."[12]

Most who knew Dostoevsky at the time agree that he ardently championed the oppressed, of which there were many in Russia.[13] The emancipation of the serfs was hotly discussed by members of the Durov circle. Dostoevsky believed that such a change would have to be instituted from above, rather than brought about by a revolt from below: one contemporary, Miliukov, reported that when "someone expressed doubt about the possibility of freeing the serfs through legal means, F[yodor] M[ikhailovich] answered sharply that he did not believe in any other way." Some testimony suggests, however, that Dostoevsky did not totally exclude violence as a last resort. Orest Miller reports that "Palm remembers that once when discussion focused on the question of 'well, and what if emancipating the serfs turned out to be impossible by any other means than revolt?' Dostoevsky with his usual ardor had exclaimed, 'then even if by means of revolt!'"[14] Although Dostoevsky and his friends may have had strong feelings on this issue, their involvement remained theoretical.

In 1856, reflecting on his earlier participation in politically subversive activity, Dostoevsky wrote that he had been "found guilty of intent (but nothing more) to act against the government."[15] As many of Dostoevsky's fictional heroes discover, the intent or desire to do something often does not result in the act being performed, even if external circumstances do not interfere. Would Dostoevsky have ever translated his outrage at social injustice into overtly revolutionary acts? Semenov-Tian-Shansky evaluates the writer's revolutionary potential as follows: "Dostoevsky never was and could not have been a *revolutionary*, but as a man of feeling he could become carried away by feelings of indignation and even ire in the face of violence committed against the humiliated and insulted ... Only in the heat of such moments was Dostoevsky capable of going out onto a square waving a red banner, something that, for that matter, nobody in the Petrashevsky circle even dreamed of."[16] His passionate nature notwithstanding, Dostoevsky does not seem to have had the makings of a revolutionary. When Maikov was trying to persuade Dostoevsky to withdraw from Speshnev's conspiracy, he reminded his friend that he was not businesslike enough to be a successful political activist.

In later life, Dostoevsky naturally had to be careful not to compromise himself or others by revealing specific information about his past involvement in subversive activity. But he thought about his own rebellious past, especially as he wrote *The Devils*, a novel in which he depicts the new breed of revolutionary which emerged in the 'sixties. Dostoevsky was particularly fascinated by Sergei Nechaev, an anarchist whose goal was to execute the tsar and whose tactics involved assuring the loyalty of his followers by implicating them all in a murder. In his article, "One of the Contemporary Falsehoods," Dostoevsky directly contrasts Nechaev and his cohorts to the Petrashevtsy, who naturally appear to be noble in comparison. But he adds: "I could never have become a *Nechaev*, but a *follower of Nechaev*, I do not vouch for it, but I may, perhaps, have become... in the days of my youth."[17] Here, Dostoevsky tentatively suggests that, had circumstances been different, he could perhaps have been led to violence. But, in a sense, Dostoevsky here reveals more about his present state than his past: he is clear about one thing, that the possibility of violent acts existed only in his youth. Separating him from his youth was what he refers to as the "rebirth of [his] convictions," which caused him to regard as an infection the socialist causes, under whose aegis he had become involved in subversive activity.[18]

Upon his return from exile, Dostoevsky's politics were considered to be conservative. Many familiar with the views and works of this later Dostoevsky find it hard to believe that Dostoevsky could have once been engaged in seditious activity, especially any motivated by or even associated with socialist ideals. For example, Dmitri Merezhkovsky writes that Dostoevsky "nearly died for that in which he not only did not believe but which he hated with every fiber of his soul."[19] Dostoevsky indeed grew to despise many socialists who, in the 'sixties and 'seventies, seemed to carry on the Petrashevtsy's struggle to ameliorate the lot of the people. But the term hatred does not fit Dostoevsky's attitude to socialism in the 'forties.

Dostoevsky espoused socialism less ardently than many of his fellow

Petrashevtsy. Antonelli's report on the final gathering at Petrashevsky's closes with a description of how one guest complained that Dostoevsky had not made sufficient use of Petrashevsky's library and had not read Fourier and other socialist thinkers.[20] Dostoevsky may not have been an expert on Fourier (as he points out in his deposition, this requires plowing through many tomes, for which he apparently had neither the patience nor the desire), but he was conversant in the teachings of Fourier and other socialist writers. Miliukov, a participant in the Durov circle, reports that "we all studied the socialists but far from all of us believed in the possibility of a practical realization of their plans. F. M. Dostoevsky was among the latter group. He read socialist writers but his response to them was critical."[21] If he failed to show great enthusiasm for socialism as a system, it was not for want of knowledge but rather due to disenchantment with what he did know. In particular, Dostoevsky is reported to have believed that there was no point in trying to apply the dreamy theories of Western socialists to the Russian reality where peasants already cooperated amongst themselves and communal institutions already existed.[22]

Although Dostoevsky conjectured that life in a Fourierist phalanstery (of which Petrashevsky and others dreamed) would be worse than penal servitude,[23] he still honored Fourier for the "love of humanity" with which his teachings were instilled. Furthermore, Dostoevsky did believe in certain causes, such as the emancipation of the serfs, which were, at the time, strongly associated with the socialist teaching of Fourier and others. In their official documents, the authorities blamed the Petrashevtsy's subversive behavior on the deleterious effect of the political ideas of the socialists and communists, citing in first order their belief in "granting equality to all human beings on the face of the earth."[24] Within Russia, the translation of this idea into action meant emancipating the serfs.

For many of the Petrashevtsy, the concomitant of socialist views was religious freethinking, if not outright atheism. When Antonelli reported what was said at Petrashevsky's on the subject of religion, the authorities concluded that the group was a threat not only to the autocracy but to Russian Orthodoxy as well. One member of the Petrashevsky group, Timkovsky, told his interrogators that his fellow-Petrashevtsy's statements on religion "at first horrified him and then completely shook his faith so that he soon arrived at the point of a political rejection of the Christian faith."[25] He reported that Petrashevsky and others had denied the divinity of Christ and the authenticity of the Holy Scriptures.

The investigation focused particular attention on a speech delivered on March 11th, 1849, by a teacher, Feliks Toll, in which he argued that religion "was not only not necessary socially but even harmful." Toll had echoed views that had gained currency among Western social thinkers of the time. Religion, suggested Toll, capitalized on man's sense of helplessness and fear in the face of nature, whereas greater control of natural forces would reduce man's fear, free him of religious sentiment and allow him to realize his full human potential.[26] Not having been at Petrashevsky's on the night this speech was given, Dostoevsky could not comment on it when asked about it during the investigation. This is unfortunate since Dostoevsky's testimony on this subject may have shed light on his religious views, which, given his personal reticence, he naturally publicized even less than he did his political views. (In his response, he did, however, manage to suggest that not all Petrashevtsy agreed with Toll's speech: he says he heard about it from Filippov who "took exception to it.")

Both those who argue that Dostoevsky remained devout and those who suggest that his faith had lapsed have set forth evidence to support their views. For example, his friend Yanovsky depicts Dostoevsky as having always been a religious man. He reports that in 1847 and 1849 Dostoevsky prepared to take communion, a process which in the Russian Orthodox Church involves fasting, confession and attending services.[27] On the other hand, from the evidence that Petrashevsky's household was known as a place where Lenten fasting was not observed and that on Good Friday of 1849 Dostoevsky attended a gathering at Petrashevsky's, the scholar Dolinin concludes that "it is apparent that he was at any rate not very steadfast in his Orthodoxy."[28] In Belinsky's letter to Gogol, which Dostoevsky read at Durov's and Petrashevsky's, Belinsky attacks the Russian Orthodox Church for having been "the mainstay of the knout and the abettress of despotism," in other words, for having gone along with a regime that promotes injustice. In defending himself for having read this letter, Dostoevsky declares that he disagreed with the "exaggerations" found therein. Still, the fact that he circulated this letter implies that freethinking was not totally alien to him. In the letter, Belinsky attacks the Church as a formal institution, without touching on questions such as the divinity of Christ or the immortality of the soul, which had been divisive when Belinsky and Dostoevsky had been friends.

During this period, he may have questioned the Church's alliance with the regime, he may not have followed the letter of the law and he may have engaged in some freethinking himself, but none of this appears to have altered his desire for faith in Christ. In fact, being exposed to opposing arguments may even have strengthened Dostoevsky's faith, which, by his own account, seemed to feed, somewhat perversely, on evidence that might be expected to undermine faith. In 1854, in a letter to Fonvizina, one of the Decembrist wives he had met while in exile, Dostoevsky wrote: "I have been a child of the age, a child of disbelief and doubt and will be one (I know) unto the very grave. What terrible torment this desire for faith has cost me and costs me now, this desire which is all the stronger in my soul, the more opposing arguments there are." For Dostoevsky, belief in Christ in no way hinged on rational criteria. "If someone were to prove to me," writes Dostoevsky, "that Christ is outside of the truth and if it *actually* were the case that the truth is outside of Christ, then I would rather remain with Christ than with the truth."[29] In this letter, Dostoevsky admits that his faith was not always strong. But, given the nature of his faith, the rational, freethinking talk of the Petrashevtsy certainly did not threaten his faith as it had threatened that of Timkovsky.

While awaiting execution, Dostoevsky took comfort in his Christian faith. Like all but one of his co-defendants, Dostoevsky did not confess to the priest who was on hand, but Lvov reports that he went up to Speshnev and said: "Nous serons avec le Christ," to which Speshnev replied: "Un peu de poussière."[30] Like Speshnev, Petrashevsky took this opportunity to deprecate eternal life. He told Mombelli, who was tied to a stake, "to lift [his] feet higher or else [he'd] arrive in heaven with a cold."[31] Dostoevsky may have gone along with the politics of Speshnev and, to a certain degree, Petrashevsky, but he adopted neither their atheism nor their materialism.

Dostoevsky's association with socialist ideology did leave its mark on his theology. In discussing Dostoevsky's religious views, Georges Florovsky emphasizes the influence of "early French socialism." He credits Fourier and George Sand with having revealed to Dostoevsky the "fateful problems posed by social issues."[32] In his later understanding of Christian love, Dostoevsky incorporated his early concern with social issues. For Dostoevsky, to love one's neighbor meant not only harboring positive sentiments toward him but also actively manifesting those sentiments through deeds. Dostoevsky believed that man's ultimate goal was to be delivered from physical necessity and death. At the same time, he recognized that earthly, fallen existence was subject to certain physical laws. In his literary works, Dostoevsky explored the tragic effects of these laws. (Money, a dramatic focus in many his works, stands as the convenient symbol of modern man's subjection to physical necessity.) Dostoevsky's active concern with social issues during his early years may have been what safeguarded him against spiritual idealism. In later life he never regarded man as a disembodied spirit. Vladimir Solovyov, the Russian theologian with whom Dostoevsky shared many views, believed that French socialists such as Fourier had done Christianity a service by "proclaiming the rehabilitation of matter." The Church (which all along had been preaching the bodily resurrection) had been reminded that matter plays a key role in the divine economy.[33] For Dostoevsky, spiritual questions were always tied up with material ones; for example, he was especially interested in how physical suffering affects the spirit. Dostoevsky roundly rejected the materialism of the socialists but by no means did he turn his back on the material aspects of existence.

In the 'seventies, Dostoevsky would occasionally show a certain nostalgia for the socialism of the 'forties. For example, writing in *Diary of a Writer* in 1877, he refers to a passage from *Anna Karenina* in which Stiva Oblonsky and Levin are out hunting and fall into a discussion of social and economic injustice. Dostoevsky notes with dismay that issues, which a few decades before had been passionately debated by the fifty or so Russians acquainted with the ideas of Fourier and Saint-Simon, had now become so hackney that they were being discussed by the likes of Stiva Oblonsky. What galled Dostoevsky (and Tolstoy) was the fact that these questions were being decided by "a person who himself did not give a farthing about the welfare of the proletarian or poor peasant, but, on the contrary, who would fleece him if given the chance."[34] Although they may have been misguided in many ways, the small group of men who first discussed the plight of the peasants in the 'forties had at least been genuinely committed to helping them. Dostoevsky occasionally exhibits a certain pride at having been in the vanguard of a movement that began with the socialists of the 'forties, for he seems to attribute to them the emergence of a social conscience in Russia. Certainly, Christianity as Dostoevsky understood it promoted an active concern with human welfare; but the socialists of the 'forties appear to have formulated this concern with winning immediacy.

When Fourier and Fourierists were attacked in the press in the 'seventies, Dostoevsky at times found himself jumping to the defense. Responding to such an attack by the military publicist Rotislav Fadeev, Dostoevsky wrote in his notebook: "No, I am for Fourier... I even underwent punishment partly because of Fourier... and I long ago renounced Fourier but I shall still come to his defense. It pains me that the thinker-general treats the poor socialist with such superiority. That is, that [Fadeev supposes that] all these learned men and youth, all these believers in Fourier are all such fools that all they need would be to come to Rotislav Fadeev and be wised up on the spot."[35] Dostoevsky felt he must answer Fadeev's charges that Fourier and Fourierists were utter nincompoops. Dostoevsky continued to credit the socialists of the 'forties with intelligence as well as good intentions and love for humanity. Where, then, had they gone wrong?

Writing in 1873, Dostoevsky noted that the utopian socialists of 'forties had prepared "darkness and horror" for humanity "under the guise of renewal and resurrection."[36] These socialists used the same salvific terminology as the Church, a fact which Dostoevsky often emphasizes in his discussion of socialism. He implies that the socialists were guilty of catachresis of the most dangerous sort: their false use of words such as "resurrection" and "renewal" had led Dostoevsky and others like him into temptation. Only after his arrest and the ordeal that followed did he begin to see that the alterations of human existence undertaken by the socialists were purely external. What was needed, Dostoevsky came to believe, was a spiritual transformation such as that promoted by Christianity. The socialists' linguistic falsehood, their bastardization of the word, was something which Dostoevsky, as a writer, took seriously and that he found hard to forgive.

In Dostoevsky's reminiscences about the period in which he was, as he puts it, "infected" by socialist views, Belinsky figures symbolically as the source of corruption. Dostoevsky declares that it was Belinsky who "initiated him into the full *truth* of this coming 'renewed world' and into the full *holiness* of the future communist society."[37] (Here, as elsewhere when he writes about socialism, Dostoevsky uses italics and quotation marks to signal the socialists' abuse of soteriological language.) In the following passage,

which culminates a section of *Diary of a Writer* devoted to Belinsky,
Dostoevsky describes how he was initiated into *another* truth and renounced
Belinsky's teaching. In the process, he encodes a description of the "rebirth of
convictions" which he underwent. Dostoevsky writes:

> During the last year of his life, I no longer visited [Belinsky]. He had taken a dislike
> to me; but I was an ardent convert to his teaching. Still a year later, in Tobolsk, as we sat in
> the stockade of a transit prison, awaiting our further lot, the wives of the Decembrists
> pleaded with the guard of the stockade and arranged for a secret meeting with us in his
> quarters. We saw these great sufferers, who had willingly followed their husbands to
> Siberia. They had abandoned everything: social status, riches, connections and family,
> sacrificing everything for the highest moral duty, for the most free duty that could exist.
> Not guilty of anything, for twenty long years they had borne everything that their
> convicted husbands had borne. The meeting lasted an hour. They gave us their blessing
> for our new journey, made the sign of the cross over us and presented each of us with a
> Gospel—the only book allowed in the stockade. For four years it lay under my pillow in
> prison camp. I read it from time to time and read it to others. I used it to teach one convict
> to read. Around me were the very people who, according to Belinsky's belief, *could not* not
> commit their crimes and who, consequently, were justified and only more unfortunate
> than others. I knew that the whole Russian people also called us "unfortunate" and I had
> heard this term a multitude of times from a multitude of mouths. But here was something
> else, not at all what Belinsky had talked about and what is heard, for example, now in
> certain verdicts of our jurors. In this word "unfortunates," in this sentence of the people
> could be heard another idea. Four years of prison camp were a long schooling; there was
> time for me to become convinced...[38]

At first, this paragraph may appear to be haphazardly constructed:
Dostoevsky sketches the demise of his relations with Belinsky and then
jumps in an apparent *non sequitur* to a more detailed description of how he
met with the wives of the Decembrists. A logical connection may exist
between Dostoevsky's association with Belinsky and his conviction to prison,
since Dostoevsky tended to blame his own involvement in subversive activity
on Belinsky's teaching. As critics have noted, Dostoevsky takes artistic license
when he presents Belinsky as his godfather in socialism, for he had been
initiated into socialism before he met Belinsky.[39] Belinsky was certainly one
of socialism's most eloquent spokesmen in Russia. Dostoevsky recognized
that Belinsky had wielded the salvific metaphors with great skill and although
he may not have converted Dostoevsky personally, he did convert countless
others, advancing the cause of liberalism. Blaming Belinsky for his arrest
clearly makes a better story. In a certain sense, this story is not pure
fabrication, since the simple fact that Dostoevsky had been sentenced largely
for his reading of Belinsky's letter may have made the causal connection
between Belinsky and prison quite immediate in Dostoevsky's mind.

But more important in this passage than the blame Dostoevsky assigns
to Belinsky is the opposition he establishes between Belinsky and the
Decembrists' wives. For Dostoevsky, these women, because they had
voluntarily sacrificed themselves, embodied Christian freedom, the very
principle which Belinsky denied. Earlier, in his profile of Belinsky,

Dostoevsky had noted that Belinsky denied "the moral responsibility of the individual" and along with it the individual's freedom. Dostoevsky now reminds the reader of this denial by mentioning that Belinsky maintained that crime was determined by external circumstances outside of the individual's control. But he, Dostoevsky, as a result of the blessing of the Decembrists' wives, reinforced by the "long schooling" received in prison camp, learned to disagree with Belinsky's determinism. Dostoevsky suggests that the new understanding he reached was an affirmation of human freedom, the principle embodied by the Decembrists' wives and taught in the Gospel they gave him.

In retrospect, Dostoevsky considered the error of the socialists—of Belinsky and of many of the Petrashevtsy (who accepted Fourier's notion that human existence follows mathematical laws)—to have been their spiritual denial of human freedom. When he emerged from exile, Dostoevsky began to see the drama of human history largely as a conflict between freedom and determinism, with Christianity often representing the former and socialism the latter. The Christian seeks an inner, freely-willed transformation of the soul, whereas the socialist attempts to inflict change from without.

In the 'forties, the struggle between free will and determinism apparently had not occupied Dostoevsky's mind in an explicit fashion. He was concerned, however, with the issue of artistic freedom. In some ways, the struggle he underwent for artistic self-determination betokens the philosophical opposition which occupied so much of his thought later in life. In his deposition, Dostoevsky touches on the subject when he identifies two forces which encroached on his freedom by attempting to determine the content of his works. First of all, he discusses how the official censorship attempted to dictate what he wrote. Then, in his separate discussions of his relations with Belinsky and Petrashevsky, he notes that relations with each of them were strained because of literary disagreement. Both Belinsky and Petrashevsky seemed to have disapproved of what Dostoevsky wrote and wanted to assign to art an idea, to make it propaganda that would preach to people. Dostoevsky maintained, on the contrary, that artistic merit should be the writer's major concern. Both the oppressive regime and "liberals" such as Belinsky and Petrashevsky were trying to determine the course of his art and eliminate his freedom as a writer.

Back in the 'forties Dostoevsky had begun to feel that liberal ideology could become something of a straightjacket. Nevertheless, he shared many of the liberals' dreams and adopted their causes. Although he clearly resented anyone's attempts to tell him what to *write*, he seemed to be unconsciously seeking something or someone that would tell him what to *do*. The young Dostoevsky appears to have felt that he was floundering. Some revealing self-analysis can be found in a letter Dostoevsky wrote to his brother: "I am only able to show that I am a man with heart and feeling when the external, when circumstance, when an event tears me by force from my habitual rottenness. Until that time I am vile."[40] Speaking of this period to his wife years later,

Dostoevsky expressed a similar view. He told her: "I would have gone out of my mind had there not been the crisis that broke my life in two. An idea presented itself to me before which my health and concern about myself appeared to be trivial."[41] When Dostoevsky became involved in political activity, he found a much-needed outlet, an escape from himself.

Dostoevsky underwent the ordeal that resulted from his political activity with surprising equanimity. He seems to have fulfilled his own prophecy about needing external circumstances to force him to prove his mettle. His letters from the fortress show his concern for others and a lack of self-pity, whereas, previously, when objectively speaking it would have seemed that there had been less to complain about, he complained more. Under interrogation, Dostoevsky, in his own words, "conducted [him]self honorably, did not foist the blame on others and even sacrificed [his] own interests when he saw the opportunity for shielding others from harm..."[42]

Dostoevsky's testimony consists of his deposition, dated May 6th, 1849, in which he answers general questions posed to him during his first interrogation and of his written answers to specific questions posed to him later, as the investigation proceeded and concerted attempt was made to determine who said what when. Dostoevsky's deposition, where his pen was allowed freer rein, provides an interesting glimpse into the author's mind. Dostoevsky, who later became known for his predilection for fictional first-person narratives of a confessional sort, here was called upon to write his *own* confession. He was clearly aware of what was at stake (his life) in making himself understood to his judges. (All they knew of him at that stage came largely from Antonelli's reports in which, ironically, Fyodor Dostoevsky is mistakenly called Petr Dostoevsky.) Dostoevsky asks them: "Who has seen the inside of my soul? Who has determined the degree of perfidy, damage and rebellion that I am charged with? On what scale was this determination made?" Dostoevsky's concern with epistemology here is characteristic, for his literary works also explore this question of how one gains knowledge of the soul. Dostoevsky implies that his judges have clearly not seen the inside of his soul and thus are not yet qualified to judge him. And given his secretive personality (which he mentions in his deposition), the testimony of others will also not be valid. The task of elucidating the inside of Dostoevsky's soul can thus only be performed by himself (or the Almighty).

But to what extent does this deposition give an accurate glimpse into Dostoevsky's soul? Years later, in describing the Petrashevtsy's attitude as they stood awaiting an execution that they believed would actually take place, Dostoevsky notes that "the overwhelming majority of us would have considered it a disgrace to renounce our views."[43] Throughout the lengthy investigation, they had also tried not to "disgrace" themselves in this way. To Dostoevsky's credit, he did his best in his deposition to represent his true views. What he says about literature and censorship, about Russia's unique historical destiny, about Petrashevsky, about Fourierism was all basically genuine. Perhaps the most overt misrepresentation of his views occurs when he disavows all sympathy for Belinsky's letter to Gogol. (Even so, in criticizing the letter, he focuses on its tone—which he may indeed have found objectionable—more than on its content. Although the letter contained opinions on religion that Dostoevsky probably rejected, the other opinions, on governmental corruption, corporal punishment and serfdom, appealed to him more than he wanted his judges to know.)

In his answers to specific questions, Dostoevsky attempts to mitigate the guilt of his associates. When commenting on compromising statements made by guests at Petrashevsky's and Durov's, Dostoevsky offers his interrogators psychological insights aimed at convincing the court that subversive behavior resulted not from true revolutionary commitment but rather from human foibles: from vanity (Petrashevsky), from youthful exuberance (Filippov), from quixotism (Timkovsky).[44]

In what Dostoevsky wrote for the Investigatory Commission, elements of his style, familiar to the readers of his artistic works, become more exaggerated. For example, in order to include in his testimony everything he could to vindicate the accused, Dostoevsky resorts to some byzantine digressions. His syntax becomes frantic and strained as he piles up clauses and phrases in an attempt to convey the proper nuance. His use of qualifying words, phrases and clauses becomes particularly pronounced. In this instance, form and content merge, since what he was engaged in writing was essentially all *qualification* of potentially compromising statements and acts.

The verdicts pronounced on Dostoevsky and other Petrashevtsy suggest that they failed in their attempts to vindicate themselves. It may even be argued that they would have been found guilty, no matter what. (Petrashevsky in his testimony intimated that they were all being tried in accordance with a judicial system modelled on that of Richelieu who declared: "Give me ten words, written by the hand of the accused and I will convict him of a crime that calls for the death penalty.")[45] Nevertheless, the conviction of the Petrashevtsy was not automatic. Apparently, their oral and written testimony had convinced the Investigatory Commission that they were not *as* guilty as Liprandi held. When the Commission had finished its work in August of 1849, it heard the opinion of Liprandi, in which the latter asserted that the Petrashevsky circle constituted "not so much a petty and isolated conspiracy as *an all-embracing plan for a popular movement, for a revolt and destruction.*"[46] The Commission persisted in denying that "an organized propaganda society" had been uncovered: "although there had been *unsuccessful* attempts to create one, although individual persons had wanted to become propagandists and some actually were, still neither the prudent, perspicacious surveillance by Mr. Liprandi of all of Petrashevsky's actions, ... nor the repeated interrogations to which the defendants were submitted, ... nor the four months of imprisonment, ... nor the sincere repentance of many, led to any such discovery [of an organized propaganda society]."[47] The case was then turned over to a Military-Judicial Commission, which was presented with summaries of all the testimony. The defendants were given the opportunity to add to their testimony in the "Signed Statements" they presented to the Military-Judicial Commission. Verdicts were then reached, but final sentencing was turned over to the General-Auditoriat, a move which surprised many. The General-Auditoriat concurred with the Investigatory Commission that "all the meetings, generally characterized by a spirit that went against the government and by a desire to change the existing order of things, did not manifest any unity of action; nor did they belong to a network of organized secret societies."[48] In other words, the authorities' conclusions partly matched what Dostoevsky and others had been telling them all along.

But the acts that the Petrashevtsy had admitted to, such as Dostoevsky's reading of Belinsky's letter, were themselves considered criminal. The General-Auditoriat determined that if military law were to be followed to the letter, then all twenty-one defendants deserved death sentences (whereas the Military-Judicial Commission had suggested that only fifteen of the defendants be executed). But, at the same time, the General-Auditoriat recognized mitigating circumstances and suggested that the Tsar commute the sentences, which he did.

In the behavior of the authorities a dual purpose manifests itself: they wanted to make an example of the Petrashevtsy and at the same time they wanted to minimize the threat posed by the Petrashevtsy in order to demonstrate how successfully the Russian autocracy had protected itself against the rebellious spirit that had overcome the rest of Europe. The Petrashevtsy case was taken as proof that official attempts to restrain the thought, conversation and reading of Russian subjects were justified and even needed to be intensified. In its concluding statement, the General-Auditoriat suggested, in particular, that tighter control be exerted over what was taught in educational institutions, that the import of foreign books be more carefully monitored, that censorship within Russia be made stricter and that police surveillance of public meetings and gatherings be increased.[49]

In essence, the story of Petrashevsky case illustrates Custine's summation of the plight of the thinking man in Russia. The Petrashevtsy wanted to ameliorate the lot of their fellow men, but society offered them no means of doing so. They gathered together privately to share their thoughts. But since in Russia at the time, "to think [was] to revolt" and "to converse [was] to conspire," they ended up as criminals. Their crimes were primarily of a verbal or ideological nature. Even the Speshnev group, which wanted to replace words with acts, remained "verbal" in its orientation. The instrument of revolution to which Dostoevsky and his cohorts had finally resorted was a printing press. (In this sense, they differed from the Decembrists who, as military men, had acted through the army.)

On December 22, 1849, Dostoevsky, whose existence up until that point had in different ways focused on the word, whether written, spoken or thought, was forced to experience. He and his comrades were told that they had been sentenced to death by execution and before being informed of the Tsar's mercy, they were forced to undergo "at least ten horrible, unbearably harrowing minutes of awaiting death."[50] Yet, even in the throes of such an experience, Dostoevsky recalled a literary precedent: Lvov reports that Dostoevsky, in a nearly ecstatic state, referred to "Le Dernier Jour d'un condamné a mort," Victor Hugo's work recording the interior monologue of a prisoner awaiting execution.[51]

These ten minutes radically altered Dostoevsky's life and his art. This experience of (as Dostoevsky put it) being "face-to-face with death" and then being "alive again" made him value being alive as never before: "Life is a gift, life is happiness, each minute could have been an eternity of happiness. *Si jeunesse savait!* [If youth knew!] Now, changing my life, I am being reborn into a new form." In the midst of this overwhelming joy at being alive, Dostoevsky felt regret: "the head that created, lived the higher life of art, that recognized and grew accustomed to the higher demands of the spirit, that head has already been cut off from my shoulders. What remains is memory and images created and not yet embodied by me." What Dostoevsky is essentially saying is that this experience was tantamount to linguistic extinction. He means this on various levels: he refers to the fact that his conviction interrupted his career as a professional writer and also to his fear that he would not even be able to write for himself while in penal servitude. But, in addition, he suggests that the experience itself transformed him so completely that it changed his relationship to language.

What Dostoevsky went through as a result of the Petrashevsky affair did not, as we know, mean linguistic extinction for him. What Dostoevsky experienced in a sense defied words and yet he had immediately set about trying to describe it in the letter he wrote to his brother. And, indeed, throughout the rest of his life, he went on giving indirect verbal accounts of this experience. Condemnation to death, understood both literally and metaphorically, figures prominently in Dostoevsky's mature works.[52] Having himself apprehended death and having felt himself transformed by the experience, Dostoevsky expressed what he had learned in artistic form, hoping, perhaps, to enact change in his reader as well.

This close brush with death and its aftermath, the period spent in what he called the "house of the dead," also radically accelerated the development of Dostoevsky's mature artistic style, of what has been called his "fantastic realism." Dostoevsky seems to have first recognized this quality, which he later developed in his own writing, in Hugo's *The Last Day of a Man Condemned to Death*, the work which he recalled as he awaited execution and which he quoted in the letter written to his brother describing his experience.[53] In the introduction to one of his later works, Dostoevsky discussed the "fantastic" premise of Hugo's work, whereby it was assumed that "a man condemned to death could (and had the time) to take notes not only on his last day but even in his last hour and literally in his last minute." Fantastic as such a premise is, it was justified, for "had [Hugo] not allowed such a fantasy, the work itself could not have existed—the most real and realistic of all the works he wrote."[54] Dostoevsky, of course, was in a position to judge whether or not Hugo's work depicts the truth. As a result of his experience on December 22nd, 1849, Dostoevsky's writing took on a new dimension, for he himself had, in a sense, become an embodiment of the literary device employed by Hugo. Dostoevsky's subsequent works are written with an eschatological awareness. When he depicts life, death is always hovering over the picture, its proximity being what gives his prose much of its intensity and tension. After experiencing those ten harrowing minutes of being face-to-face with death and after relating them to himself and others, Dostoevsky, as an artist, went on to concentrate on depicting the invisible movements of the soul in moments of psychic intensity, the most dramatic of these being times in which death is apprehended. The eschatological bent taken by Dostoevsky's thought produced a literary style with the concomitant urgency and immediacy.

In participating in the rebellious talk of the Petrashevsky group and its offshoots, Dostoevsky failed to bring about the social changes he had dreamed of. But his failure in this sphere contributed, indirectly, to his becoming a truly revolutionary figure. The realm which he revolutionized was literary rather than political. Through his writing, Dostoevsky sought to transform his readers by challenging the existing order in their souls and, in the process, he developed a literary style that was innovative, if not downright revolutionary.

Notes

1. "Perepiska Nikolaia Pavlovicha s shefom zhandarmom A. F. Orlovym" in *Petrashevtsy*, Moscow, V. M. Sablin, 1907, p. 151. Also quoted in F. M. Dostoevskii, *Polnoe sobranie sochinenii*, Leningrad, Nauka, 1972-present, XVIII:320. [For subsequent references to this edition of Dostoevsky's works the abbreviation *PSS* will be used.]

2. Liprandi, the member of the Ministry of the Interior who launched the investigation, contrasted the Petrashevsky group to the Decembrist group which consisted primarily of members of the gentry, most of whom were also military men. Liprandi considered the social heterogeneity of the Petrashevsky group to be a sign that it was getting ready to mobilize all levels of society. See: "Otryvok iz mneniia deistvitel'nogo statskogo sovetnika Liprandi," *Petrashevtsy* (1907), p. 15.

3. Stepan Dmitrievich Ianovskii, "Vospominaniia o Dostoevskom," in *F. M. Dostoevskii v vospominaniiakh sovremennikov*, Moscow, Khudozhestvennaia Literatura, 1964, I:168-169. (Although many have questioned the validity of Yanovsky's reminiscences on the grounds that his political conservatism kept him from understanding Dostoevsky's politics of the time, this

particular anecdote seems to give a genuine summary of Dostoevsky's views of the Petrashevsky circle at the time. Dostoevsky joined other groups because he had become frustrated by the Petrashevsky circle where people, it seemed to him, only *played* at being liberal. Dostoevsky wanted to to do more: he wanted to enact new ideas.)

4. [Report of the General Auditoriat to Tsar Nicholas], *Petrashevstsy: Sborniki materialov*, P. E. Shchegolev, ed., Gosudarstvennoe Izdatel'stvo, Moscow-Leningrad, 1926-1928, III:3-4.

5. Astolphe de Custine (Marquis), *The Empire of the Czars*, London: Longman, 1843, I:168.

6. Petr Petrovich Semenov-Tian-Shanskii, "Memuary" in *F. M. Dostoevskii v vospominaniiakh sovremennikov*, Moscow: "Khudozhestvennaia literatura," 1964, I:216.

Dostoevsky makes much the same point in *Diary of a Writer* when he notes that "an extraordinarily large number, in comparison to those who stood on the scaffold, but who were just as much 'Petrashevtsy' as we were, remained completely untouched and undisturbed. Of course, they never even knew Petrashevsky but Petrashevsky was not the crux of the matter..." Dostoevskii, *PSS*, (XXI:129.)

7. These feuilletons appeared in the *St. Petersburg Gazette* (Sanktpeterburgskie vedomosti) on April 27th, May 11th, June 1st and 15th of 1847. Their text appears in *PSS*, XVIII:11-34.

8. The use Dostoevsky makes of "Aesopian language" in these feuilletons to convey frustration at the state of affairs in Russia is discussed by Joseph Frank in *Dostoevsky: The Seeds of Revolt, 1821-1849*, Princeton: Princeton University Press, 1976, pp. 217-228.

9. N. L'vov, "Zapiska o dele petrashevtsev," *Literaturnoe nasledstvo*, V. V. Vinogradov, ed., Moscow: Akademiia Nauk SSSR, 1956, 63:171.

10. See, for example: V. Leikina, *Petrashevtsy*, P. E. Shchegolev, ed., Moscow, 1924, p. 40.

11. The authorities found a copy of a document to be signed by members of a "Russian society" who had to commit themselves to bear arms and "take full and open part in the rebellion and fighting." The text of this document appears in *Petrashevtsy* (1907), p. 34.

12. In his memoirs, Dostoevsky's friend and doctor, Yanovsky, describes how Dostoevsky seemed to have become tormented by his friendship with Speshnev. Dostoevsky spoke of being beholden to Speshnev. Yanovsky sensed that Dostoevsky had something more in mind than a monetary debt when Dostoevsky said to him: "Don't you understand, that from that point on I've had a Mephistopheles of my own?" *Dostoevskii v vospominaniiakh sovremennikov*, I:172.

13. See, for example: Orest Miller, "Materialy dlia zhizneopisaniia F. M. Dostoevskogo" in *Biografiia, pis'ma i zametki iz zapisnoi knizhki F. M. Dostoevskogo*, St. Petersburg: A. S. Suvorin, 1883, pp. 90-91.

14. Miller, p. 85.

15. *PSS*, XXVII (Book 1): 224; Letter 107, to E. I. Totleben, March 24th, 1856.

16. *Dostoevskii v vospominaniiakh sovremennikov*, I: 211.

17. *PSS*, XXI: 129.

18. Dostoevsky referred to the "rebirth of [his] convictions" in the same article of 1873 in which he suggested that he may have become a follower of Nechaev (*PSS*, XXI: 134). Soon after emerging from penal servitude, Dostoevsky began to speak of this radical change which had taken place within him. For example, in a letter of 1856, referring to his past politics, he wrote that "ideas and even convictions change, the whole man changes..." (*PSS*, XXVIII [Book 1]: 225).

19. Dmitrii Merezhkovskii, *L. Tolstoi i Dostoevskii*, St. Petersburg, 1903, I: 112. As quoted in: N. F. Bel'chikov, *Dostoevskii v protsesse petrashevtsev*, Moscow: Nauka, 1971, p. 89.

20. *Delo petrashevtsev*, Moscow-Leningrad: Izdatel'stvo Akademii Nauk SSSR, 1951, III: 442.

21. P. Miliukov, "Fedor Mikhailovich Dostoevskii" in *F. M. Dostoevskii v vospominaniiakh sovremennikov*, I: 185.

22. Miller, pp. 91-92.

23. Ibid.

24. Shchegolev, ed., *Petrashevtsy*, III: 11.

25. Timkovsky's testimony is quoted in A. Dolinin, "Dostoevskii sredi petrashevtsev,"

Zven'ia, Moscow-Leningrad: Academia, 1936, p. 521.

26. The text of Toll's speech can be found in Schegolev, ed., *Petrashevtsy,* II: 163-66.

27. Miller, pp. 94-95.

28. A. Dolinin, "Dostoevskii sredi petrashevtsev," VI: 526. Dolinin also refers to Yanovsky's evidence that Dostoevsky took communion but he discounts Yanovsky as an unrealiable source (VI: 525).

29. *PSS,* XXVIII (Book 1): 176. Letter 90, to N. D. Fonvizina, January-February, 1854.

30. *Literaturnoe nasledstvo,* 63: 188.

31. Ibid.

32. Georgii Florovskii, *Puti russkogo bogosloviia,* Paris: YMCA Press, 1983, 3d edition, p. 297.

33. Florovskii, p. 309.

34. *PSS,* XXV: 55.

35. *PSS,* XXI: 265.

36. *PSS,* XXI: 131.

37. *PSS,* XXI: 131.

38. *PSS,* XXI: 12.

39. Joseph Frank discusses what he calls the "irresistibly hagiographic version of the great drama of [Dostoevsky's] conscience" (whereby Belinsky is regarded as the source of Dostoevsky's corruption) in *Dostoevsky: The Seeds of Revolt,* pp. 182-198.

N. F. Bel'chikov examines the evidence that Dostoevsky was sympathetic to socialism before he met Belinsky in : *Dostoevskii v protsesse petrashevtsev,* Moscow: Nauka, 1971, pp. 57-64.

40. *PSS,* XXVIII (Book 1): 139. Letter 71, to M. M. Dostoevsky, January-February, 1847. Quoted in Miller, p. 73.

41. Miller, p. 112.

42. *PSS,* XXVIII (Book 1): 224. Letter 107, to E. I. Totleben, March 24, 1856.

According to one story he told, Dostoevsky was offered clemency by General Rostovtsev, a member of the investigation committee, if he would agree to tell all; when he refused, Dubbelt, another member, turned to Rostovtsev and said: "I told you so" (Miller, pp. 106-107).

43. *PSS,* XXI: 133.

44. Victor Terras discusses Dostoevsky's use of psychology in his defense in *The Young Dostoevsky,* The Hague: Mouton, 1969, p. 276.

45. *Literaturnoe nasledstvo,* 63: 183.

46. *Petrashevtsy* (1907), p. 15.

47. Quoted in *PSS,* XVIII: 327.

48. Quoted in *PSS,* XVIII: 327-28.

49. Shchegolev, ed., *Petrashevtsy,* III: 288.

50. *PSS,* XXI: 133.

51. *Literaturnoe nasledstvo,* 63: 188.

52. Eventually, Dostoevsky began to see the death sentence and reprieve inflicted on him as a kind of parable, with the death sentence representing man's mortality and the reprieve, resurrection into eternal life.

53. "On voit le soleil!", the exclamation Dostoevsky uses to express his joy at being alive, is an echo of Hugo's condemned man's words. (See notes in *PSS,* XXVIII [Book 1]: 450-451.)

54. Dostoevsky compares the premise of this work to that of his own "The Meek One" (1876), which is also an interior monologue. (*PSS,* XXIV: 6.)

BIBLIOGRAPHY

I. Documents relating to Dostoevsky's case. (Russian)

Bel'chikov, N. F. *Dostoevskii v protsesse petrashevtsev*. Moscow: Nauka, 1971.

Delo Petrashevtsev. Moscow-Leningrad: Izdatel'stvo Akademii Nauk, 1937-1951. 3 volumes.

Dostoevskii, Fedor Mikhailovich. Volume 18 of *Polnoe sobranie sochinenii v tridtsati tomakh*. Leningrad: Nauka, 1978.

Evgrafov, V. E., editor. *Filosofskie i obshchestvenno-politicheskie proizvedeniia petrashevtsev*. Moscow: Gosudarstvennoe izdatel'stvo politicheskoi literatury, 1953.

Petrashevtsy. (Politcheskie protsessy nikolaevskoi epokhi.) "P. Sh.", editor-compiler. Moscow: V. M. Sablin, 1907.

Shchegolev, P. E., editor. *Petrashevtsy: Sborniki materialov*. Moscow-Leningrad: Gosudarstvennoe izdatel'stvo, 1926-1928. 3 volumes.

II. Memoirs relating to Dostoevsky's involvement in the Petrashevsky affair. (Russian)

F. M. Dostoevskii v vospominaniiakh sovremennikov. (Compiled by A. Dolinin.) Moscow: Izdatel'stvo khudozhestvennoi literatury, 1964. (The memoirs by S. D. Ianovskii, A. P. Miliukov, P. P. Semenov-Tian-Shanskii and D. D. Akhsharumov found in Volume 1 relate to the Petrashevsky affair.)

L'vov, F. N. "Zapiska o dele petrashevtsev" (with notes by M. V. Butashevich-Petrashevskii) in *Literaturnoe Nasledstvo*, V. V. Vinogradov, ed. Moscow: Izdatel'stvo Akademii Nauk SSSR, 1956. 63:165-190.

III. Works discussing Dostoevsky's involvement in the Petrashevsky case. (Russian).

Bel'chikov, N. F. "Dostoevskii i Petrashevtsy" in *Dostoevskii v protsesse petrashevtsev*. Moscow: Nauka, 1971. pp. 5-90.

Dolinin, A. "Dostoevskii sredi petrashevtsev" in *Zven'ia: Sborniki materialov i dokumentov po istorii literatury, iskusstva i obshchestvennoi mysli XIX veka*. Moscow-Leningrad: Academia, 1936. 6:512-545.

Fridlender, G. M. *Realizm Dostoevskogo*. Moscow-Leningrad: Nauka, 1964.

Kirpotin, V. Ia. *F. M. Dostoevskii: Tvorcheskii put' (1821-1859)*. Moscow: Gosudarstvennoe izdatel'stvo khudozhestvennoi literatury, 1960.

Leikina, V. R. *Petrashevtsy*. Moscow: Obshchestvo politicheskikh katorzhan i ssyl'no-poselentsev, 1924.

Miller, Orest. "Materialy dlia zhizneopisanii F. M. Dostoevskogo" in *Biografiia, pis'ma i zametki iz zapisnoi knizhki F. M. Dostoevskogo*. St. Petersburg: A. S. Suvorin, 1883, pp. 1-176.

IV. Works discussing Dostoevsky's involvement in the Petrashevsky case. (English).

Frank, Joseph. *Dostoevsky: The Seeds of Revolt, 1821-1849*. Princeton: Princeton University Press, 1976.

——. *Dostoevsky: The Years of Ordeal, 1850-1859*. Princeton: Princeton University Press, 1983.

Grossman, Leonid. *Dostoevsky: A Biography*. Translated by Mary Mackler. London: Allen Lane, 1974.

Mochulsky, Konstantin. *Dostoevsky: His Life and Work*. Translated by Michael A. Minihan. Princeton: Princeton University Press, 1967.

Monas, Sidney. *The Third Section: Police and Society in Russia under Nicholas I*. Cambridge: Harvard University Press, 1961.

Terras, Victor. *The Young Dostoevsky (1846-1849): A Critical Study*. The Hague-Paris: Mouton, 1969.

Dostoevsky's Statement on the Petrashevsky Affair

I have been told to relate all that I know about Petrashevsky and the people who attended the Friday gatherings at his house; that is, I have been told to give testimony about the facts and my personal opinions of these facts. Judging from my first interrogation, I conclude that a detailed response to the following items is required of me:

1. What is Petrashevsky like as a man, in general, and as a political figure, in particular?
2. What took place at the gatherings at Petrashevsky's that I attended and what opinions do I have of those gatherings?
3. Did the Petrashevsky group have some hidden, clandestine purpose? Is Petrashevsky personally a dangerous man, and to what extent does he pose a threat to society?

I have never been on very close terms with Petrashevsky, although I attended his Friday gatherings and he, in turn, would call on me. Ours was an acquaintance which I did not prize very highly, since we lacked common ground both in our personalities and in many of our views. And this is why I maintained relations with him only to the extent required by courtesy—that is, I visited him from month to month and sometimes even less. I had no reason to break off relations with him entirely. And besides, it was sometimes interesting for me to attend his Friday gatherings.

I was always struck by the great eccentricity and peculiarity of Petrashevsky's behavior. As a matter of fact, I owe our acquaintance to the fact that his peculiar behavior piqued my curiosity from the very first time I saw him. However, I seldom went to his house. At times, six months would elapse without my going there. During last winter, from September on, I was not at his house more than eight times. We have never been on close terms with each other and I think that during the whole time we have been acquainted we have never been left alone with each other, face-to-face, for more than half an hour. I definitely noticed that when he would stop by my house, it was as if he were performing an act of courtesy, whereas, for instance, it would be painful for him to carry on a lengthy conversation with me. And I felt the same way;

for, I repeat, we had little common ground, either in our ideas or in our personalities. We avoided getting involved in lengthy discussions with each other, because from the tenth word we would have started to quarrel, and both of us were fed up with that. It seems to me that our respective attitudes toward each other were the same. At any rate, I know that I very often went to his Friday gatherings not so much for his sake or for the sake of the gatherings themselves as for the sake of seeing certain people whom I knew and liked but saw extremely rarely. But, in any event, I have always respected Petrashevsky as an honest and noble man.

Many people—almost all who know Petrashevsky or have heard of him—talk about his eccentricities and peculiarities, and they even pass judgment on him on this basis. I have heard it said several times that Petrashevsky has more brains than sense. To be sure, it would be difficult to account for much of his peculiar behavior. Often, when you run into him on the street and ask where he is going and why, he gives you some peculiar answer, describes some very peculiar plan that he is en route to carry out, and leaves you at a loss as to what to make of the plan and of Petrashevsky himself. At times he will go to such pains over some inconsequential matter that you would think his whole fortune depended on it. At other times, he will be rushing off somewhere for half an hour in order to wrap up some "trifling matter," whereas wrapping up that "trifling matter" would actually take two years. He is a man who is forever fussing and moving about; he is forever busy with something. He reads a lot; he admires Fourier's system and has studied it in detail. In addition, he is very involved in studying law. This is all I know about him as a private person, on the basis of data sorely lacking for a completely accurate judgment of someone's character, for, I once again repeat, I was never on very close terms with him.

It would be hard to say whether Petrashevsky (regarded as a political figure) has any particular ideological system of his own or some particular point of view on political events. As far as I could tell, his views were consistent only in regard to one system; and it was not even his own but that of Fourier. It seems to me that Fourier is actually what keeps him from looking at things in an original way. Yet I can quite definitely say that Petrashevsky is quite far from believing in the possibility of an immediate application of Fourier's system to our social reality.[1] Of that I have always been convinced.

The group that gathered at Petrashevsky's on Fridays consisted almost entirely of his close friends and old acquaintances; at least, that was my impression. Of course, new faces would appear, but, as far as I could tell, this happened rather rarely. Some of the others I know simply because I happened to talk with them three or four times a year; and, finally, many of Petrashevsky's guests I hardly know at all, even though I have been seeing them at the Friday gatherings for as much as a year or two by now. But, even though I do not know all the people well, I have lent an ear to their various opinions. By and large, these opinions were all discordant; one would contradict the other. I met with no unity whatsoever in the Petrashevsky group, no orientation, no common cause. One can positively say that three among them could not be found who would all agree on any given subject. Hence the endless arguments among one another; the endless contradictions and differences of opinion. I even took part in a few of these arguments myself.

But before I tell on what account I entered into these arguments and on what specific subjects I spoke, I will say a few words about the charges leveled against me. Essentially, to this very moment I still do not know what the charges against me are. I was simply informed that I took part in the general discussions at Petrashevsky's, that I spoke *like a freethinker,* and, finally, that I read aloud the literary article "Belinsky's Corrspondence with Gogol." I will say in all sincerity that there has been nothing harder for me in all the world than defining the word: *freethinker, liberal.*[2] What is meant by this word? A person who speaks unlawfully? But I have seen people for whom admitting to having a headache amounts to acting unlawfully, and I know that there are likewise others who are ready to shout from the rooftops whatever their tongue is capable of cranking out. Who has seen the inside of my soul? Who has determined the degree of the perfidy, damage, and rebellion that I am charged with? On what scale was this determination made? Perhaps the charges are based on a few remarks I made at Petrashevsky's? I spoke there three times: twice about *literature* and once on a subject totally unrelated to politics, on *individuality* and *human egoism.*[3] I cannot recall that there was anything political or freethinking in my remarks. I cannot recall that at Petrashevsky's I ever spoke my mind *completely, revealing myself as I actually am.* But I know myself, and if the charge is based on some remarks that had been jotted down on a scrap of paper and were seized during a raid, well, I am not afraid even of such a charge, although such a charge is the most dangerous kind, there being nothing more damaging, incoherent, and unjust than some remarks taken from God knows where, relating to God knows what, overheard hastily, understood hastily—or more often than not completely misunderstood—and jotted down hastily. But I repeat: I know myself and am not afraid of even such a charge.

Yes, if *seeking the better* is liberalism, *freethinking,* then, in this sense, perhaps, I am a freethinker. I am a freethinker in the very same sense in which one can call any man a freethinker who in the depths of his heart feels that he has the right to be a citizen, feels that he has the right to seek the welfare of his country, because in his heart he finds both love for his country and the knowledge that he has never in any way done it harm. But did this *seeking the better* address the realms of the possible or of the impossible? Let it be proven that I ever sought changes and upheavals in a violent, revolutionary way, or that my seeking ever aroused bile and hatred! But I am not afraid of the evidence; for no allegation in the world will take anything away from me or add anything to me; no allegation can cause me to be other than I actually am. Did my freethinking manifest itself in the fact that I spoke aloud about things about which others consider it their duty to be quiet—not because they want to avoid saying something against the government (this would not even cross their minds) but because, in their opinion, the subject is one about which it is unbecoming to talk out loud? Was this my "freethinking"? I've always even taken offense at this fear of speaking out, which is more likely to be an insult to the government than pleasing to it. And, in fact, why should the righteous man be fearful for himself and what he says? For this is tantamount to supposing that the laws do not sufficiently protect the individual and that one can be ruined by mere words, by careless phrases. But why is it that we ourselves have so conditioned everyone to regard as an eccentric act any remarks that in any way resemble an opinion and are made openly and out loud! My feeling is that if we all were more frank with the government we ourselves would be much better off. It has always grieved me to see how we are all as if instinctively fearful of something, to see how when we gather together in a crowd in some public place we eye each other mistrustfully, gloweringly, cast sidewise glances and act suspicious of people. Or else how when someone starts to talk, say, about politics, he is sure to start to speak in a whisper and with the most secretive look, even though the notion of a republic may be as far from his head as France. People will say: "Certainly, it is to our advantage that in Russia we do not shout everything from the rooftops." Of course, this cannot be denied; and yet excessive suppression and excessive fear give our everyday life a somber coloring, presenting everything in a joyless, forbidding light; and what is most distressing of all, this coloring is false; for all this fear is groundless and pointless (of this I am convinced), all these apprehensions are nothing more than our invention, and we ourselves only pointlessly alarm the government with our secretiveness and mistrustfulness. And this strained state of affairs often results in much ado about nothing. The most ordinary remarks, spoken out loud, gain inordinate significance, and the event itself— the fact that the remarks were ever made—by reason of its perceived eccentricity, often takes on colossal proportions and is bound to be attributed to extraneous (extraordinary) causes rather than to the actual (ordinary) ones. I have always been convinced that a conscious belief is better and stronger than an unconscious one that is unstable, wavering, ready to topple over at the first wind to blow. Consciousness is something that you cannot hatch or develop on silence. It is we ourselves who try to avoid universalization; we split up in circles or else petrify in our isolation.[4] And who is to blame for this state of affairs? We ourselves and nobody else—so I have always thought.

Although by way of example I did mention our discussions on social issues, I myself am actually far from beind a loudmouth, as anyone who knows me will corroborate. I do not even like speaking in public and at length, even among friends, of which I have few, and especially at social gatherings, where I have the reputation of being a quiet, taciturn, unsociable man. I have a very small circle of acquaintances. Half my time is taken up by the work that supports me; the other half is regularly taken up by illness and the hypochondriacal attacks that I have been suffering for already three years now. There is scarcely any time left for reading and finding out what is going on in the world. Very little time is left for friends and acquaintances. And so, if what I wrote just now opposed the system of universal and seemingly systematic suppression and secretiveness, it was written because I wanted to voice my conviction and not at all in order to defend myself. But what are the charges against me anyway? That I spoke about politics, the West, censorship, and so on? But who in our day has not spoken and thought about these issues? Why was I educated, why has a desire for knowledge been aroused in me by learning if I do not have the right to voice my personal opinion or disagree with that opinion which retains its authority no matter what? In the West a terrifying spectacle is taking place, an unprecedented drama is being played out.[5] The age-old order of things is cracking and shattering. At every moment the most fundamental principles of society threaten to collapse, sweeping the whole nation with them as they fall. Every day, thirty-six million people risk all their future, their property, their own existence and that of their children, gambling on it all as if they were at a card game! How could such a sight not attract attention and stimulate curiosity and a desire for knowledge, how could it not harrow one's soul? This is the very same land that gave us learning, education, and European civilization; such a spectacle serves as a lesson! It is, after all, history, and history teaches us about the future. Given these circumstances, is it conceivable that we will be prosecuted—we who received a certain degree of education, in whom was aroused a hunger for knowledge and learning—is it conceivable that we will be prosecuted for having had whatever curiosity it takes to talk occasionally about the West, about political events, to read current books, to keep an eye on the developments in the West and even to study them as much as opportunity allows? Is it conceivable that I will be prosecuted for paying rather serious attention to the crisis that is causing unfortunate France to wince and nearly be cast asunder, and for considering, perhaps, this crisis to be historically necessary in the life of that nation, as a transitional stage (who can determine this at present?) that eventually will result in a better time? My freethinking about the West and about revolution never went beyond this opinion or similar ideas. And if I did talk about the upheaval in France, if I did take the liberty to form an opinion on current events, does it follow that I am a freethinker, that I am of republican persuasion, that I am an opponent of the autocracy, that I am trying to undermine it? Impossible! For me there never was anything more absurd than the idea of republican rule in Russia. My views on this score are familiar to all who know me. Ultimately, such an accusation would run counter to all my beliefs and to my education. Perhaps I will go a bit further in trying to explain the revolution in the West and the *historical necessity* of the current crisis there. For many centuries, for more than a millennium, a very persistent struggle has dragged on there between society and the authority that has imposed itself onto an alien civilization by means of conquest, violence and oppression.[6]

And what about here in Russia? Our country did not take shape along Western lines.[7] We have historical examples in front of us: 1) the fall of

Russia to the Tatars as a result of the weakening and disintegration of authority; 2) the disgrace of the Novgorod republic—a republic tried out for several centuries on Slavic soil; and finally, 3) the twice-told salvation of Russia, thanks solely to the strengthening of the autocracy: Russia saved the first time from the Tatars and the second time during the reforms of Peter the Great, when her warm, childlike faith in her great helmsman—and nothing else—enabled her to survive such a drastic transition to a new life. And, for that matter, who here in Russia even thinks about a republic? And if indeed reforms do lie in store, it will be clear as day even for those who seek them that these reforms must stem from the authority itself, which will have to be even further strengthened while the reforms take place; for otherwise the whole matter would have to take place by revolutionary means. I doubt that a champion of a Russian revolt could be found in Russia. Examples are known and remembered to this day, although they took place long ago. In conclusion, I call to mind remarks of mine that I have made more than once: from Peter the Great on, all that has been good in Russia has invariably originated from above, from the throne, whereas to this day nothing other than obstinacy and ignorance has manifested itself from below. This opinion of mine is quite familiar to many of the people who know me.

I spoke about censorship, about its inordinate severity in our time, and I lamented this fact; for I felt that some misunderstanding had taken place, resulting in a strained state of affairs that was hard on literature.[8] It saddened me that in our day the calling of the writer has been debased by some dark suspicion and that, from the outset, even before he has written anything, the writer is regarded by the censors as if he were some natural enemy of the state, and they set to picking apart his manuscript with unmistakable prejudice. It saddened me when I heard that a work had been prohibited not because it was found to contain anything that was considered liberal, freethinking, or counter to morality, but simply because the story or novel had too unhappy an ending, because it presented too somber a picture, even if the picture did not accuse anyone or insinuate anything about anyone in society, and even if the tragedy resulted from incidental and external factors. Let them pick apart everything that I have written, published and unpublished, let them examine the manuscripts of my already published works, and they will see what they were like before being submitted to the censorship—let them try to find so much as a single word counter to morality or to the established order of things. Yet, as a matter of fact, I myself have been the victim of such a prohibition, simply because the picture was painted in too somber colors. But if only the censors knew what a somber situation the author of the prohibited work confronted! He was faced with the necessity of going worse than without bread for three whole months since the work provided my means for survival. And, on top of everything, in the midst of the deprivation, grief, and near despair (for, financial considerations aside, it was painful to the brink of despair to see one's creation, which one loved—which had cost one labor, health and one's best spiritual energy—prohibited because of a *misunderstanding,* because of *suspicion*), so then, on top of everything, in the midst of deprivation, grief, and despair, one still has to find enough relaxed, cheerful hours in which to produce a new literary work in colors that would be light, rosy, and pleasing. And one has no choice but to write such things, since one has to survive. If I spoke, if I complained a little (oh, but I complained so very little!), does this mean that I engaged in freethinking? And what was I complaining about? a misunderstanding. Namely: I was beating my brains out trying to prove that every writer is suspect in advance, that he is regarded with distrust and wariness, and I blamed the writers themselves for not wanting on their own to take the initiative in seeking a resolution for this baneful misunderstanding. Baneful, because such a strained situation threatens the very existence of literature. Whole art forms will have to disappear: already satire and tragedy can no longer exist. Given the severity of today's censorship, writers such as Griboedov, Fonvizin, and even Pushkin can no longer exist.[9] Satire ridicules vice, more often than not vice parading under the guise of virtue. But nowadays how can there be any kind of mockery whatsoever? The censor sees insinuations in everything; he suspects that there is some personage depicted, that there is gall, that the author is insinuating something about some concrete person or some situation. I myself—having cast off my sadness—would very often chuckle over what the censor found *to be a threat to society* and unsuitable for publication in my manuscripts or in other people's. I laughed because nowadays such suspicions would not cross the mind of anybody but a censor. In the most innocent, clean sentence the most criminal of thoughts is suspected, the censor obviously pursuing it with great intellectual exertion as an eternal, immutable idea that cannot leave his head, that he himself, shaken by fear and suspicion, created, that he himself incarnated in his imagination, that he himself colored with fantastic, terrifying colors, ultimately destroying his phantom together with the innocent cause of his fear—the writer's sinless original sentence. As if simply by hiding vice and the somber side of life one hides from the reader the fact that vice and the somber side of life exist on earth! No, an author will not succeed in hiding the somber side by systematically omitting it from the reader's eyes, but rather he will only make his readers suspect him of insincerity and untruthfulness. For that matter, is it possible to depict things using only light colors? How can the light part of a picture be perceptible without the somber? Can a picture exist without both light and shadow together? If we have a conception of what light is, it is only because such a thing as shadow exists. We are told: "depict nothing but valor and virtue." But it's impossible to identify virtue without vice; the very concepts of *good* and *evil* have resulted from the fact that good and evil have always coexisted, side by side. Just imagine what would happen if I were to present ignorance, vice, abuse, arrogance, violence! The censor would immediately be suspicious of me and think that I was speaking about everything in general without exception. I am not championing the cause of the depiction of vice and the somber side of life! Neither the one nor the other is dear to me. I speak simply in the interest of art.

Observing, having finally become convinced, that a misunderstanding had arisen between literature and censorship (and a misunderstanding and nothing else), I lamented, I prayed that this sorry misunderstanding would soon come to an end; because I love literature and cannot not care about it; because I know that literature is one of the reflections of the life of nation, that it is a mirror of society. Together with education and civilization, new concepts arise that require a Russian definition and name in order to be passed on to the people; for, under the present circumstances, the task of naming them does not fall to the people, since civilization comes not from them but from above; the concepts can be named only by the society that received civilization before the people, that is, the upper layer of society, the class already prepared for the reception of these ideas. Who then formulates the new ideas in such a form that the people will be able to grasp them—who then if not literature? Peter the Great's reform would not have been so easily accepted by a people that did not understand what was required of them. And what was the Russian language like at the time of Peter the Great? It was half Russian and half German, because half of German life, German ideas, and German customs were grafted onto Russian life. But the Russian people do not speak German, and the appearance of Lomonosov immediately after Peter the Great was not a chance occurrence.[10] Without literature, there can be no society; but I observed that literature was declining and, for the tenth time, I repeat, the misunderstanding that has arisen between literature and the censors tormented me, tortured me. I spoke, but I spoke only about harmony, about an accord, about the obliteration of a misunderstanding. I did not ignite anyone around me *because I had faith.* And besides, I spoke only with my closest friends, with my fellow writers. Is this harmful freethinking?

I am being charged for reading the article "Belinsky's Correspondence with Gogol" at one of the gatherings at Petrashevsky's. True, I did read the article, but would the person who informed on me be able to say to which of the correspondents I was more partial? Let him recall whether there was in my judgments (from which I refrained)—or even in the intonation of my voice, or in my posture during the reading—anything that could in any way demonstrate my partiality to one party in the correspondence over the other? Of course, he cannot say that there was. Belinsky's letter is written in too strange a way to evoke a sympathetic response. Rebukes repel the heart rather than attract it, and the whole letter is crammed with rebukes and written with gall. Ultimately, the whole article is a model of lack of substantiation—a fault tht Belinsky could never get rid of in his critical articles and that became more pronounced as his mental and physical powers dwindled in the course of his illness. These letters were written in the last year of his life, during his stay abroad. For a while I was on rather close terms with Belinsky.[11] As a man, he was an outstanding human being. But the illness that led him to his grave even managed to crush the human being in him. It embittered and hardened his soul and flooded his heart with gall. His imagination, deranged and strained, magnified everything so that it would take on gigantic dimensions and show him things that he alone was capable of seeing. Faults and vices suddenly developed that there had been no trace of when he was a healthy man. He developed a sense of conceit that made him extremely prickly and touchy. At the journal, which officially listed him as a contributor but for which because of illness he worked only very little, the editors tied his hands and would not assign him very important articles. This hurt him. And such was his state of mind when he wrote his letter to Gogol. My quarrel and final break with Belinsky in the last year of his life are no secret to a lot of people in the literary world. The cause of our falling-out is likewise common knowledge: it happened over ideas about literature and the orientation literature should take. My view was radically opposed to Belinsky's view. I reproached him for striving to give literature a function that was limited and unworthy of it, that reduced it to mere description (if I may so express myself) of *nothing more than newspaper facts* or scandalous occurrences. Specifically, I protested that one does not win anybody over with gall and that, on the contrary, one merely bores each and every one to death by seizing on every Tom, Dick and Harry in the street, buttonholing every passerby and starting to preach to him by force and to lecture him until he is at his wit's end. Belinsky lost his temper with me and, eventually, our coolness developed into a formal quarrel, the result being that finally we did not see each other at all during the last year of his life. I had wanted to read those letters for a long time. In my eyes, this correspondence is a rather remarkable literary monument. Both Belinsky and Gogol are very remarkable people. Their mutual relations are extremely fascinating, all the more so for me since I knew Belinsky. Petrashevsky happened to catch sight of the letters in my possession and asked: "What is that?"; and I, not having had the time to show him the letters then and there, promised to bring them to his house on Friday. I myself had volunteered and was then naturally obligated to keep my word. I read the article as neither more nor less than a literary monument, firmly convinced that it could not lead anyone into temptation, even though it was not totally devoid of a certain literary merit. As for myself, I was literally not in agreement with a single of the exaggerations found therein. Now I ask that the following circumstances be taken into account: Would I have gotten it into my head to read a piece by somebody with whom I had broken precisely over ideas and nothing else (this is no secret; it is a known fact to many) and, what is more, a piece written during his sickness, while he was in a state of mental and spiritual disorder—would I have gotten the notion into my head of reading this piece, presenting it as a model, as a formula that ought to be followed? I have only now realized that I made a mistake and that I ought not to have read the article out loud; but at that time it did not even dawn on me that I should not read it, for I did not have the slightest inkling of possible charges against me, I did not have the slightest inkling that I was doing anything sinful. Out of respect for someone already dead, who had been remarkable in his time, and whom many revere because of several articles on the aesthetics of literature written with a truly great understanding of literary matters, and also out of a sensitivity resulting from our ideological quarrel, which was a fact known to many—for these reasons, I read the whole correspondence, restraining myself from making any comment and maintaining utter impartiality.

I mentioned that I spoke in public about politics, censorship, and so forth. But I was only groundlessly incriminating myself. I just felt like having a chance to express my train of thought. But never did I speak about these things at Petrashevsky's. I spoke at his place only three times or, more accurately, twice. Once about *literature* in connection with an argument with Petrashevsky over Krylov,[12] and the other time about *individuality* and *egoism*. On the whole, I am not a very talkative person and I do not like speaking out when there are people present that I do not know. My pattern of thought and my true nature are known only to very few of my friends. I avoid big arguments and prefer to give in simply in order to be left alone. But I was provoked to this literary argument, the subject of which, on my part, was the notion that art has no need of orientation, that it is an end unto itself, that an author ought only to trouble himself with achieving artistic merit and the idea will come on its own; for artistic merit presupposes an idea. *In a word, it is obvious that this orientation is diametrically opposed to the journalistic and incendiary.* It is also been obvious to many that this has been my orientation for several years. What is more, everybody at Petrashevsky's heard our quarrel; everybody can corroborate what I have said. The upshot was that it turned out that Petrashevsky and I shared the same convictions about literature but had not understood each other. Everybody also heard this denouement. And I noticed eventually that the whole argument had stemmed partly from conceit, because I had once doubted whether Petrashevsky had any coherent knowledge on the subject. And as for what concerns the second topic: about *individuality* and *egoism,* well, I wanted to demonstrate that among us there is more *ambitiousness* than true human dignity, that we ourselves are sinking into self-disparagement, into disintegration of the individual as a result of petty conceit, egoism, and the futility of our activities. This topic is strictly psychological.

I have said that among the group that gathered at Petrashevsky's there was not the slightest coherence, the slightest unity either in thought or in outlook. It seemed to be one big argument that had begun at one point in order never to end. It was in the name of that argument that the group gathered—for the sake of arguing and arguing things into the ground; after almost every time people would disperse in order to renew the argument the next time with renewed energy, feeling that not even one tenth of what they wanted to say had been said yet. Without arguments, things would have been incredibly dull at Petrashevsky's, because arguments and disagreements were all that was capable of uniting these diverse people. The talk was about everything and nothing in particular; and the talk was the same as in any circle that has gotten together casually. I am convinced of this. And if I occasionally took part in the arguments at Petrashevsky's, if I went to his house and was not alarmed when I heard some heated remarks, well then it was because I was totally convinced (and remain convinced to this very day) that what went on there was of a domestic nature, among a circle of Petrashevsky's mutual acquaintances and friends, and not of a public nature. Such was actually the case, and if presently such inordinate attention is being directed at what went on at Petrashevsky's, it seems to me that this has been due to Petrashevsky's being widely known to nearly all of Petersburg for his peculiarities and eccentricities. And so, for this very same reason, his gatherings have likewise become widely known; and I know for a fact that all the talk has exaggerated their significance, even though the talk of the town contained more mockery of Petrashevsky's gatherings than alarm about them. The fact that the discussion there was sometimes rather frank (but it was always in the form of a misgiving, and what was said always developed into an argument) did not disturb me. Because, in my opinion, it is better for some fiery paradox, some misgiving to be aired in front of others (of course, not at the marketplace but in a circle of friends) rather than remaining locked inside a person without outlet, only to grow hard and become petrified in his soul. A shared argument is more useful than isolation. The truth always rises to the surface, and common sense carries the day. This is how I looked on those meetings, and in this spirit I would sometimes go to Petrashevsky's. And experience proved me right. Because, for example, people finally stopped talking about Fourierism since Fourierism had been showered with ridicule from all sides, even as a doctrine. And if someone at Petrashevsky's were to have gotten it into his head to broach the subject of the application of Fourier's system to our social reality, people right then and there would have laughed in his face, without the slightest beating around the bush. I say this because I am utterly convinced of the truth of what I say.

In answer to the question as to whether the Petrashevsky group had some hidden, clandestine purpose, it can definitely be said that, bearing in mind all the difference of opinion, all the confusion of ideas, characters, personalities, professions, all the arguments, going to the brink of hostility but still remaining nothing more that arguments—bearing all that in mind and taking it all into account, it can definitely be said that it would have been out of the question for there to have been some hidden, clandestine purpose in all that chaos. There was not even a shadow of unity and could not have been till kingdom come. And although I did not know everybody in Petrashevsky's group or everything about it, still, judging from what I saw, I can say for a fact that I am not mistaken.

Now I have to answer the final question, the answer to which will constitute the conclusion of my vindication. Namely: is Petrashevsky personally a dangerous man, and to what extent does he pose a threat to society? When this question was put to me the first time I was not able to give a direct answer. Before considering this question, I had to resolve for myself a whole series of questions and misgivings that immediately cropped up in my mind, that I was unable to resolve right there on the spot, that required a certain amount of thought; and, for this reason, I stood there not knowing what to answer. Now, having pondered everything, I will present both my preliminary thoughts and, finally, the answer to the question I had been asked, an answer I came to as a result of those thoughts.

First, if I was asked whether Petrashevsky poses a threat to society, I take it to mean primarily as a Fourierist, as a follower and promoter of Fourier's doctrine. I was shown a notebook covered with small writing and I was told that I probably would recognize the handwriting. I am not familiar with Petrashevsky's hand; we never corresponded, and I did not have the slightest idea that he would launch himself into authorship. And I say this in all earnestness. This is why I know absolutely nothing about Petrashevsky as a Fourierist propagator. All that I am familiar with are his scholarly views. And even so, he and I seldom, almost never, engaged in a scholarly discussion of Fourier, for our discussion would have immediately turned into an argument. He knew this perfectly well. Petrashevsky never imparted to me any plans or instructions and I certainly do not know whether or not he had any. What is more, even if he had some, which I absolutely do not know, he, not being at all on close terms with me and in general not full of goodwill, would in all likelihood (of this I am sure) have hidden everything from me and would not have made known a single word to me. And, as far as I am concerned, I never had the slightest desire to be a party to his secrets. And so I can not say a thing about Petrashevsky as a Fourierist, except from a strictly scholarly point of view.

I know that Petrashevsky has great respect for Fourier's system. As a Fourierist, of course, he cannot help but want people to agree with him. But I was asked: is he making disciples? *Is he luring teachers from various educational institutions in order, having converted them, to work through them to spread Fourierism among the young?*[13] My answer: I can give absolutely no response to this question because I do not have sufficient data since I do not know Petrashevsky's secrets. I have been told that among Petrashevsky's acquaintances there are some teachers, for example, Toll. But I do not know Toll at all and found out only recently that he was a teacher. As for Yastrzhembsky, I only found that he was a teacher when he spoke about political economy. I do not know any other teachers. Being not only not on close terms but even on distant terms with Toll, I know neither the history of his acquaintance with Petrashevsky nor when they got to know each other—in a word, I had not even the slightest curiosity about these things. As far as Yastrzhembsky is concerned, I had the opportunity to learn his views on economics when I happened to hear him speak twice. As far as I could tell, he is an economist of the newest school and tolerates socialism only to the extent that the most strict professors of social science tolerate it, for socialism, for its part, has been of great benefit to social science thanks to its critical analysis and statistical aspect. Quite simply, I gather that Yastrzhembsky is far from being a Fourierist and that he has nothing to learn from Petrashevsky. But I add that I do not know Yastrzhembsky personally at all. I have *never* engaged in conversation with him and apparently he regards me in a similar fashion. I do not know the full scope of his ideas, just as he does not know mine. Thus I can only judge Petrashevsky as a promoter of doctrine on the basis of guesses, on the basis of conjectures.

But on the basis of guesses I can say nothing. I know that my deposition will not be taken as the definitive or principal word, but nevertheless it does remain a deposition. And what if I am mistaken? This mistake will lie on my conscience. I was shown a manuscript about whose existence I had no previous knowledge. I read one sentence of this manuscript. In this sentence was expressed an impassioned desire for the immediate triumph of Fourier's system. If the whole manuscript is in this same vein, if Petrashevsky acknowledged it as his, then, obviously, he did desire the propagation of Fourier's system. But whether up until now he has actually taken any measures—I do not know. I am not privy to his secrets and I think that in the final analysis I can be trusted. No one can prove that Petrashevsky and I were ever on very close terms. I went to his house on Fridays as an acquaintance and nothing more. I do not know any of his plans and that was the first time I saw the manuscript whose contents, other than one sentence, are completely unknown to me. And so, as to whether or not he has taken any measures, I cannot say. But let me take the liberty of setting forth some of my own personal thoughts, ones that make up a most deep conviction that I have been pondering a long time, thoughts which occurred to me previously in the same way as now and because of which, when first asked about Petrashevsky's guilt, I could not give a definitive answer. I am aware of the importance in the eyes of Petrashevsky's judges of evidence such as books, manuscripts, and conversations jotted down in fragments. But since I have been asked about Petrashevsky, let me take the liberty of setting forth my opinion on his whole case.

Petrashevsky believes in Fourier. Fourierism is a peaceful system; it enchants the soul with its elegance, it seduces the heart with the love for humanity that inspired Fourier as he created his system, and it delights the mind with its harmony. It attracts people not by bilious attacks but by inspiring them with love for humanity. In this system there is no hatred. Fourierism does not propose any political reform; its reform is economic. It encroaches neither on government nor on property, and at one of the last meetings of the Assembly, Victor Considérant, the spokesman of the Fourierists, solemnly renounced any encroachment on the family. Finally it is a dilettantish armchair system and will never be a popular one. All during the February upheaval, the Fourierists did not once go out into the street but instead remained in the editorial offices of their journal, where they have been spending their time for twenty-odd years, engaged in reverie about the future beauty of the phalanstery. But, without a doubt, this system poses a threat if only for the simple reason that it is a system. Secondly, for all its elegance, it is still a utopia of the most unrealistic sort. But the threat posed by this utopia, if I may take the liberty of expressing myself in this way, is rather more *comic* than terrifying. In the West there is no social system that is unpopular and mocked to such a degree as Fourier's. It would long since have died out; its leaders themselves do not realize that they are living corpses and nothing else. In the West, in France, at present, any system, any theory poses a threat to society; for the hungry proletarians, in their despair, latch onto all remedies and are ready to make a banner out of any remedy. They are at their eleventh hour. Hunger is chasing people into the streets. But Fourierism has been forgotten out of disdain, and even *Cabetism,* more ridiculous than which has never been produced on earth, evokes a lot more symphathy. But, as for what concerns us, Russia, Petersburg, well, here one has only to take twenty steps in the street to become convinced that on our soil Fourierism can only exist in the uncut pages of a book or in a soft, mild, dreamy soul, but not otherwise than in the form of an idyll or in the manner of a verse-poem of twenty-four cantos. Fourierism cannot inflict serious harm. First of all, even if serious harm were possible, its propagation would amount to a utopia, for it goes unbelievably slowly. In order to understand Fourierism completely, one has to study it; and it is a whole science. One has to plow through up to ten volumes. Could such a system ever become popular? Be spread from the lectern through teachers? Why, this is physically impossible, if only because of the scope of the science of Fourierism! But, I repeat, no serious harm can come from Fourier's system and if the Fourierist does inflict harm on anyone, it is only on himself, in the general opinion of those who have any common sense. For me, the most supreme comicality lies in *activity that is universally useless.* And Fourierism, along with any Western system, is so unsuited for our soil, so inappropriate to our circumstances, so out of character with our nation—and, also, to such an **extent** the handiwork of the West, to such an extent the product of the **Western** situation, where, at all costs, the proletarian question is being resolved—that with its urgent tenor Fourierism at present for us (among whom there are no proletarians) would be unbearably absurd. The activity of the Fourierist would be the most pointless of all and consequently the most comical. This is why, based on my *guess,* I consider Petrashevsky more clever than that and never *seriously* suspected him of anything beyond an armchair respect for Fourier. All the rest I, *in all honesty,* was ready to take for a joke. A Fourierist is an unfortunate but not a guilty man—that is my opinion.

Finally, in my opinion, not a single paradox, however many there have been, has been able to hold its ground by its own strength. This is what history teaches us. And the proof lies in the fact that in France in a single year nearly all systems collapsed, one after another; and they collapsed by themselves the moment that it came to putting theory into practice. Having taken all this into account, even if I did know (which I do not know, I once again repeat), but even if I did know that Petrashevsky, not afraid of ridicule, still strives for the spread of Fourierism, then I would still refrain from saying that he poses a definite threat. First of all, how Petrashevsky could pose a threat as a promoter of Fourierism is beyond my comprehension. He is laughable but not harmful! This is my opinion, and this is what my conscience makes me anwer to the question posed to me.

Finally, another thought has occurred to me that I cannot be silent about;

it is of a strictly practical nature. I have had an old, longstanding conviction that Petrashevsky is infected with a certain type of conceit. Out of conceit he instituted his Friday gatherings and out of conceit he did not get fed up with those Friday gatherings. Out of conceit he possessed a lot of books and, apparently, he liked it to be known that he had rare books.[14] Of course, this is nothing more than my observation, my guess, for, I repeat, all that I know about Petrashevsky I know incompletely, imperfectly, by guesses, based on what I saw and heard.

This is my answer. I have reported the truth.

F. M. Dostoevsky's Formal Interrogation

To Mr. Dostoevsky

To the preliminary points of inquiry put by the Imperially-Established Investigatory Commission you are to give brief and clear explanations in full accord with the truth:

(1) What is your name, patronymic and surname, how many years old are you, of what denomination are you and have you duly observed prescribed religious rites?

—Fyodor Mikhailov Dostoevsky, twenty-seven years old, of Orthodox, Greek-Russian denomination. I have duly observed prescribed religious rites.

(2) Identify your parents and state their whereabouts, if they are alive.

—My father was a staff-medic, the collegiate counsellor, Dostoevsky. My mother was from the merchant class. Both are dead.

(3) Where were you educated, at whose expense, and when did you complete your education?

—I was educated at the Central Engineering Institute, at personal expense. I completed my education upon graduating from the classes for officers at the Engineering Institute in 1843.

(4) Are you engaged in government service, when did you enter the latter, what post do you occupy and what rank do you hold; in addition, have you ever previously been under investigation or on trial and, if so, for what namely?

—Upon completion of the senior class for officers at the Central Engineering Institute in 1843, I enrolled in active miliatry service in the drafting office of the Engineering Department. I retired in 1844, with the rank of lieutenant. Until now I have never been under investigation or on trial.

(5) Do you own any immovable property or private capital and, if not, what means have you had for housing and feeding yourself and your family, if you have one?

—At my parents' death, I, together with all our remaining family, inherited immovable property with approximately one hundred souls in the Tula province. But in 1845 by mutual agreement with my relatives, I relinquished my due share of the estate in return for a sum of money which was received in a single payment. I have been providing for myself by means of the literary work which has been my livelihood up to present.

(6) With whom have you been on close and familiar terms and in frequent contact?

—My contact has been *completely open* with nobody except for my brother, the retired Engineer-Sub-lieutenant Mikhailo Dostoevsky. I was on friendly terms with several people; the closest of which were the family of the artist Maikov, the physician Yanovsky, Durov, Palm, Pleshcheev, Golovinsky and Filippov. I have been in frequent contact with my brother Mikhailo, with Doctor Yanovsky, who has been treating me for my illness for over two years, and with Andrei Aleksandrovich Kraevsky, on account of my close involvement in the journal he publishes, *Notes of the Fatherland*.

(7) What contact have you had with people within the Empire and abroad?

—Aside from my Petersburg acquaintances, I have been in contact with my relatives in Moscow. I have had no contact whatsoever with people abroad.

Retired Engineer-Lieutenant Fyodor Mikhailov Dostoevsky.

F. M. Dostoevsky's Testimony

[Question:] Have you been acquainted with Petrashevsky for a long time?

[Answer:] I have been acquainted with Petrashevsky for exactly three years. I saw him for the first time in the spring of 1846.

Fyodor Dostoevsky

[Q:] What prompted you to make Petrashevsky's acquaintance?

[A:] We became acquainted by chance. If I am not mistaken, I was with Pleshcheev in the café by the Politseisky Bridge, reading the newspapers. I noticed that Pleshcheev had stopped to talk with Petrashevsky but I failed to take note of Petrashevsky's face. Five minutes later I left. Before I reached Bolshaya Morskaya, Petrashevsky caught up with me and out of the blue asked me: "What is your idea for your next story, if I may take the liberty of asking?" Since I had not taken note of Petrashevsky in the café and since he had not addressed a single word to me there, I took Petrashevsky for a complete stranger who had accosted me on the street—and not for Pleshcheev's acquaintance. Pleshcheev came hurrying up and dispelled my bewilderment; we exchanged a few words and, having reached Malaya Morskaya, parted ways. In this fashion, Petrashevsky piqued my curiosity from the very first time I saw him. This first encounter with Petrashevsky was on the eve of my departure for Revel, and I did not see him again until that winter.[15] He struck me as quite an original person, but not an empty one; I was impressed by his erudition and knowledge. I did not go to his house for the first time until around Lent of 'forty-seven.

Fyodor Dostoevsky

[Q:] Did you attend his gatherings often?

[A:] During the first two years of our acquaintance, I went to Petrashevsky's very seldom. Last winter I started going to his house more often. But still only from month to month. And for that matter, it was not on a regular basis. Sometimes I would be there two weeks in a row and then let a whole month elapse before I went again. So, for instance, during the month of March I was not there a single time. I started going more often, out of curiosity; in addition, I would run into several acquaintances there. Finally, I myself sometimes took part in the discussion, in the argument which, left unfinished one evening, would unwittingly summon me to go the next time and finish the argument.

Fyodor Dostoevsky

[Q:] How many people were present at those gatherings and who among them attended the gatherings on a regular basis?

[A:] Ten, fifteen, twenty and sometimes as many as twenty-five five people.

I still do not know some of Petrashevsky's acquaintances by last name. So, for example, I only found out the last names of Akhsharumov and Berestov since being arrested. The same goes for Kropotov whom I saw, it seems to me, only once at Petrashevsky's. As for Kashin, I do not even know him by face and never saw him at Petrashevsky's. I got to know some better than others. But, in any event, not all of Petrashevsky's guests were strangers to me before I saw them there. Among those closest to me were: Pleshcheev, Durov, Palm. In addition I knew the younger Desbut, Kaidanov, Lvov, Mombelli, Balasoglo, Filippov. They were at Petrashevsky's fairly often, but I recall that they were not there every time. Kaidanov was there four times in the course of this winter, Kuzmin once, Pleshcheev, three times, not more. I barely remember the elder Desbut. He, his brother, Kaidanov and Palm hardly every took part in the general discussion. Of those taken to Petrashevsky's by me were Golovinsky and my brother. Golovinsky had been planning to go to Kazan. Petrashevsky happened to find out about this and mentioned that he would like to send a letter to Kazan with Golovinsky and I volunteered to bring Golovinsky to his house. I was able to convince Golovinsky to go because he had already heard about Petrashevsky from rumors and had once asked me about him. I took Golovinsky strictly in order to give him a chance to see Petrashevsky and his acquaintances, knowing that he would be able to go to Petrashevsky's no more than twice before his departure, in other words, knowing that because of its short duration I was foisting a boring and unpleasant acquaintance neither on the one nor on the other. Golovinsky went all of two times.

My brother, Mikhailo Dostoevsky, also met Petrashevsky through me while staying with me upon his arrival from Revel. He first saw Petrashevsky at my place and was invited by him to the gatherings; I took my brother so that he would meet people and be entertained; for when he arrived from Revel he did not know a soul in Petersburg and was lonely in the absence of his family. However, my brother never took part in the discussion at Petrashevsky's. I never even heard him say two words. All those who went to Petrashevsky's know that such was the case. He went less often than I did and if he did go, it was out of curiosity and because, being a family man, of extremely modest means, a breadwinner, who denied himself almost all forms of amusement, he could not deny himself this sole form of entertainment: keeping up with an extremely small circle of acquaintances so as to not lose all social graces by not leaving his hearth. I say this because of the fact that my brother met Petrashevsky through me, because I am to blame for this acquaintance and hence for the misfortune of my brother and his family. For, if during these two months of imprisonment I myself and others have endured boredom and anguish, then he has suffered ten times more in comparison with us. By nature, he is of weak constitution, inclined to consumption and, in additioɪ , he is beating his breast over his ruined family—which is literally and inevitabɪy bound to be ruined by anguish, deprivation and hunger in his absence. And this is why arrest for him must be literally tantamount to execution, since he is less guilty than all the rest. I considered myself duty-bound to say this; for I know that he is not guilty of anything, either in word or even in thought.

Attending most frequently of all were Chirikov, Deev and Madersky, but they lived in Petrashevsky's building.

Fyodor Dostoevsky

[Q:] It has been established that at the meeting at Petrashevsky's on March 11th Toll gave a speech on the origins of religion, arguing, among other things, that it was not only not necessary socially but even harmful. Comment on this.

[A:] I heard about what Toll said about religion from Filippov who told me that he took exception to it. I myself was not at Petrashevsky's that evening.

Fyodor Dostoevsky

[Q:] At the meeting at Petrashevsky's on March 18th, Yastrzhembsky gave a speech about the sciences during which he explained that statistics actually ought to be called not statistics but civil social science but since the Grand Duke had ordered it to be called statistics, there was nothing to be done, that was what it had to be called. Comment on this.

[A:] I was not there and did not hear about it. During the month of March, from the 1st to the 25th, I was ill and left the house only for the most pressing concerns.

Fyodor Dostoevsky

[Q:] It has been established that at the meeting at Petrashevsky's on March 25th, there was talk about the manner in which subjects should be stirred up against the authoritites. Durov argued that each person had to be shown evil at its very source, that is, in the law and the sovereign. On the other hand, Berestov, Filippov, Kaidanov and Balasoglo said that the subjugated people had to be incited against the most immediate authorities and, passing in this fashion from the lower to the higher, unwittingly, almost gropingly, be led to the very source of evil. Give commentary on this.

[A:] That time I was not at Petrashevsky's. I heard about that discussion from Filippov.

Fyodor Dostoevsky

[Q:] During that same discussion, Filippov said: "Our system of propaganda is the best and to renounce it would mean renouncing the possibility of realizing our ideas." Comment on these remarks.

The hand of an unidentified person: He was not at that meeting and therefore was not asked.

[Q:] At the meeting at Petrashevsky's on April 1st, Petrashevsky, in speaking about censorship, argued that although it tends to limit the opportunity for greater development, it nevertheless does perform the service of expunging all nonsense from a given work, granting the work a practical and orderly air; on the contrary, were censorship to be done away with, then throngs of people would appear on the scene, attracted by personal motives and desires and although they might use their talents to carve out a place in the history of literature, for all that, they might stand in the way of human progress and of the achievement of goals dear to them all. Comment.

[A:] I heard such a view from Petrashevsky.

Fyodor Dostoevsky

[Q:] At the same meeting, in the course of discussion of the emancipation of the peasants, it was said that the overriding concern of each individual ought to be to emancipate those oppressed, suffering victims, that the government cannot emancipate them since it cannot emancipate them without land; and to emancipate them with land, the landowners would have to be reimbursed, whereas the means for that are not available; were it to emancipate them without land or without paying the landowners for the land, the government would be acting in a revolutionary way; however, the manner in which the emancipation of the peasants was to be undertaken without the will of the government was not specified in these remarks. Comment on the measures intended for this purpose.

[A:] I heard the entire discussion. I recall Golovinsky's remarks; he spoke passionately, but I do not recall any definitive conclusion to the discussion in which it was said that the emancipation must come about through a revolt and I maintain that everyone dispersed without any solution whatsoever to this question. It all ended in one big argument.

Fyodor Dostoevsky

At my oral interrogation, I concurred that Golovinsky acknowledged the possibility of a sudden insurrection, initiated by the peasants acting on their own, since their tribulation already weighs heavily upon their consciousness. This was in fact what the question put to me was referring to, although I did not realize this at first. Still, I feel obliged to add that Golovinsky expressed this idea as a fact rather than as something he hoped for; for, in allowing for the possibility of the emancipation of the peasants, he is far from revolt and from a revolutionary mode of activity. This has always been my impression from conversations with Golovinsky.

Fyodor Dostoevsky

[Q:] In refuting Golovinsky's remarks, Petrashevsky said that when the peasants are emancipated a clash between classes is bound to occur, which, being disastrous in and of itself, might be even more disastrous since it would give rise to military despotism or, what is even worse,—to spiritual despotism. Comment on what was meant by military despotism and spiritual despotism.

[A:] I remember that Petrashevsky refuted Golovinsky. I cannot clearly recall Golovinsky's response, although I do remember that he went into a rather involved explanation. Perhaps I was being distracted by some other conversation at the time. Not recalling the essence of what was said, I cannot give a clear answer to this question and am therefore compelled to leave it unanswered.

Fyodor Dostoevsky

As for Petrashevsky, I recall that he spoke of the necessity of reforms: judiciary reform and reform of the censorship before peasant reform and he even calculated the advantage the serf segment of the peasants has over the free segment under our present judicial system. But I have no clear recollection of what the phrases "military and spiritual despotism" signified. Besides, Petrashevsky sometimes spoke obscurely and incoherently, such that one had difficulty comprehending him.

Fyodor Dostoevsky

[Q:] At the same meeting, Petrashevsky, in speaking about the judicial system, maintained that in our tangled, multifarious, biased judicial system justice cannot be effected and if out of a thousand cases one does arise where it is effected, then this somehow happens accidentally, by chance; that there is only one conceivable judicial system in which its goal, that is, justice, can be effected and that is a public judicial system—trial by jury. Give commentary on this.

[A:] It was said.

Fyodor Dostoevsky

[Q:] In the same discussion, Petrashevsky explained that changes in the judicial system ought not be demanded but rather most humbly beseeched since the government, whether it refuses or fulfills the request, will only worsen its position. By refusing the estate this request, it would be inciting it against itself and our cause would gain ground.[16] By fulfilling the request, the government would also weaken itself and allow the opportunity for making greater demands and, all the same, our cause would gain ground. Comment on this.

[A:] That was said. The point, in my opinion, is clear and self-explanatory.

Fyodor Dostoevsky

[Q:] At the same meeting, Golovinsky said that a change of government could not occur suddenly, that, to begin with, a dictatorship must be established. Give commentary on this.

[A:] The passage of time notwithstanding, I have tried to summon up all my recollections of that evening and while I do remember much of the discussion I can in no way remember such words being said about our government.

Golovinsky twice set about speaking for all to hear. The first time, he spoke about the urgency of the serfdom question, about the fact that everyone was actively concerned with this question and that, indeed, the plight of the peasant deserved attention. The second time, in response to Petrashevsky, he maintained his opinion that the solution of the peasant problem was more important than the demand for judiciary and censorship reform. Both times he spoke fairly briefly, the first time for no more than ten minutes and the second time for no more than a quarter of an hour; on this score my recollections are accurate and both times he began and ended with discussion about the peasants, without launching into other subjects. In such a short period he could not have touched on anything other than the topics mentioned above as having been discussed by him. Whereas in order to broach such a plank as a change of government, let alone launching into details (for if he had said that government cannot change suddenly, then the very weight of the topic would have required him to make at least a few remarks in explanation of his view; and, moreover, as it is set forth in the question put to me, he really did launch into detail because, as cited in the question, he proposed the means, that is, he said that "a dictatorship must be established" and he must necessarily, naturally have made at least a couple of remarks about what sort of dictatorship), so, I repeat, if he began to speak on this subject and by necessity launched into details, he would have been suddenly skipping from his previous topic to a completely different one; what is more, he would have begun to speak about a plank about which not a word had previously been uttered in his speech; thirdly, he would have had to have done this in connection with something, but no connection presented itself to him; finally, he would have had to speak for longer than a quarter hour or twenty minutes, for that matter. (In regard to the duration of Golovinsky's speech, I rely on the accuracy of my recollections and also on the fact that nobody will be able to prove otherwise.) Consequently, *even if something in that vein was said*, then it was said, for the aforementioned reasons, to such a degree in passing, fleetingly, *inter alia,* and with such negligible impact that it is not surprising that I should now not only have forgotten about those remarks but not even have caught them at the time of the discussion itself. Moreover, what was in fact said was not those remarks but only something similar, in that vein, for example, that such is the case *in general* during a change of any government and not our goverment, in particular.

I wrote above "even if it was said." By these words, I in no way wished to maintain that the testimony given about Golovinsky was false. Rather I merely wanted to say that these remarks of Golovinsky's (if indeed they were made) have evidently been assigned an exaggerated significance and I wished to demonstrate this by pointing out the sheer physical impossibility, the lack of time for discussion of such an important, new theme, not to mention the unexpectedness of the shift from the previous topic to this new one, arising I know neither how nor in what connection. And so, perhaps, he even said this, I cannot clearly remember, but as a remark made in passing and *in general*, and not at all as the expression of a desire for a change of our government. In one of my responses to a question put to me, I said that I knew Golovinsky personally, that I knew his ideas and never heard him voice any desire to bring his ideas into fruition by means of revolt or by any violent means whatsoever. I now again confirm that I never heard a word from him about a change of government. Golovinsky most often spoke about the status of the peasants because he was obsessed with that problem and, I recall, he never spoke on any other topic once the discussion moved in that direction. At least I never heard anything of the sort.

Fyodor Dostoevsky

Just this very moment I recalled that during one of my conversations with Golovinsky, one on one, in my apartment, we started talking about the peasants and the prospect of their emancipation. Since I was very interested in this problem, I asked Golovinsky what means he proposed for emancipating the peasants without ruining the landlords, that is, by reimbursing the landlords, submitting to him that the problem could not be resolved in any other way; for the landlord of our day had not enslaved the peasants, rather this had happened two centuries before his time, in other words, he is in no way to blame for it, whereas in losing his right to the peasant he would lose a worker and, consequently, capital. I remember very clearly that Golovinsky not only agreed with this but even told me that to his way of thinking there were no direct impediments to emancipating the peasant with reimbursement, that, on the contrary, reimbursement was viable and he even made a few comments about certain financial measures whereby, being spread over several years, the payment could be made in full. But I do not remember his specific plan since it was suggested in passing and we were interrupted.[17]

I have introduced this recollection in order to show that Golovinsky does not advocate revolutionary or any sort of violent mode of action whatsoever, that, in my *final* judgment, he is heavily involved in the peasant problem simply because this problem is interesting in itself and worthy of attention and that he dwells on peaceful measures, viable ones rather than destructive ones. Such is the Golovinsky I have come to know.

Fyodor Dostoevsky

[Q]: It has been established that at the meeting at Petrashevsky's on April 15th, Petrashevsky gave a speech on giving precedence to the question of the judicial system in which he said that in the course of changing the judicial system all other faults would also come to light and that an insurrection must not be undertaken without certainty of complete success, that changes in the judicial system can be achieved through legal means, by demanding of the government such things that it, once it realizes their justice, cannot refuse and that having achieved change in the judicial system it would be possible to demand still further changes from the government. Comment on this and give testimony as to the circumstances under which you read Belinsky's letter to Gogol at that meeting.

[A:] Since this is in accordance with Petrashevsky's ideas, it could well have been said.* After my reading, as I recall, I was off in another room with Kaidanov and Palm.

I read Belinsky's letter to Gogol having myself volunteered to do so when I had seen Petrashevsky at Durov's. I had given my word and could not go back on it. Petrashevsky reminded me of my promise when I was as the gathering at his house. However he was not aware, and had no way of being aware, of the contents of the letter. I read it, trying not to display partiality for either one or the other of the correspondents. On reading the letter, I did not talk about it with any of those who were at Petrashevsky's. Nor did I hear any response to the correspondence. During my reading, fragmentary exclamations were occasionally heard, laughter was occasionally heard, but I could not make out anything coherent from it all. Moreover, since I was involved in my reading, I cannot even say now where the laughter and exclamations I heard were coming from. I admit that I acted carelessly.

F. Dostoevsky

*Upon further reflection on the question I find myself compelled to give a certain clarification of my response. In the question, the following phrase which serves to incriminate Petrashevsky is cited: "...and that an insurrection must not be undertaken without certainty of complete success..." I answered above that all that was set forth in the question was in accordance with Petrashevsky's ideas. By this remark I simply had in mind Petrashevsky's well-known desire for changes and improvements in the judicial system,—a desire, the fulfillment of which is first and foremost in his mind.

As for the remarks about insurrection, I consider it my duty to say that I never heard from Petrashevsky about any plans for insurrection either when I was alone with him or in the midst of the general discussion, that this does not fit with what I know of Petrashevsky and so I cannot say that those remarks were also in accordance with his ideas. Since I was off in another room during his speech, I cannot say anything definitive about these remarks, but I surmise and guess that they were not made in the form of a pressing and feasible plan but simply as a statement of fact, as proof of the impossibility of any sort of armed insurrection. And I am convinced of this because I myself noticed more than once that Petrashevsky would not approve when someone, not keeping himself in check, spoke too truculently and imprudently at his gatherings. I also noticed that he always tried somehow to put a stop to such a slip and to ill-advised remarks.

But in adding this clarification I am unable, and in no way wish, to vouch for Petrashevsky as regards his secret intentions—if he has any (which I never have known), as regards his innermost thoughts. Perhaps, indeed, it behooves me to confess that I knew him far less well than I thought I knew him. I also do not intend for what I say to justify what I do know about how he thought. No; in making this clarification I am prompted solely by a sense of justice. I am bound to tell the truth. And so, I repeat that an inordinately truculent statement as, for instance, one about revolt, about armed insurrection, could not have been made by Petrashevsky *at his gathering, as an expression of his desire*, that is, in such a way that this phrase, taken by itself, in the form of a treatise about the means to insurrection and revolt, could, in turn, have served as the topic of discussion on another Friday. I affirm and again repeat that the meetings at Petrashevsky's were not of such a nature as to include discussion about means of revolt. I cannot remember even a single such speech or thought being put forth either by Petrashevsky himself or by one of the guests at his gatherings. Finally, I am firmly convinced that if Petrashevsky would have allowed himself such topics of discussion or had permitted someone else to develop such an idea, then the next Friday he would have been without guests. At least I can vouch for the people I know. Not to mention the ulterior motives and most secret plans of Petrashevsky and each of his visitors (merely assuming the possibility of the existence of such plans), not to mention them and in no way using a denial of them to justify Petrashevsky's gatherings, I want simply to say in conclusion to this clarification that Petrashevsky and his guests could not have been so imprudent as to form a *conspiracy*, even if they had wanted to (which I mention once again by no means insisting but rather by way of suggestion) in such an open, incautious and foolhardy way.

I had to make this clarification in order to be telling the truth and in order not by my previous answer to cast a dangerous and unjust shadow of suspicion on many of those who went to Petrashevsky's, whose views I know well and for whom I can even vouch.

Fyodor Dostoevsky

[Q:] Aside from these conversations which have been specified to you as having taken place at Petrashevsky's, was there anything else of note said there regarding the government and, if so, by whom?

[A:] I cannot recall a single conversation that was particularly remarkable besides those on which I have had the honor of giving commentary and which accounted for virtually all of Petrashevsky's Fridays during the past winter, beginning in October. For that matter, I can speak only for those evenings that I attended in person. Timkovsky's speech took up two or three evenings (I was at two); Yastrzhembsky spoke five evenings (I was there three times.) Finally I know secondhand that Toll and Filippov spoke and that there was also an argument about bureaucrats. After that I was there in person two evenings when literature was discussed. And after that, when the discussion was about peasants, censorship and the judicial system. Those two times I was present—and these are all the speeches and conversations that I know of, except non-political and non-serious ones; such as, for example, a few remarks made by Mombelli about the detrimental effects of cardplaying and the resulting decay of morals. According to his theory, cardplaying, by occupying the mind with false and deceptive activity, diverts it from its real essentials, from edification and from useful activities.

At Petrashevsky's, not always were "speeches" (as they have been called) pronounced: the floor was given *by and large to those* who spoke counter to the majority opinion there, in such a way that everyone who disagreed did not state their objections all at once and thus drag out or pointlessly interrupt the discussion. But, by and large, particularly after the speeches, everyone quickly broke up into small groups where there was cross conversation which is impossible to recall and, for that matter, one was not even able to catch it all at the time. A great deal of what has been presented to me for response seems to have been said during those noisy individual conversations. But let me take the liberty of making a few *general* comments about these speeches and conversations.

Since here in Russia nobody is accustomed or able to make speeches, the custom of giving speeches, instituted at the gatherings at Petrashevsky's solely in order to eliminate unnecessary noise, made everyone uneasy due to its novelty and our lack of experience. On more than one occasion I noticed that in order to gain confidence the speaker would often as if deliberately resort to certain tricks which were both out of character and contrary to his wont. One such trick was that of the biting turn of phrase, the remark made for comic effect, the libellous remark, the gibe, the truculent opening sally. When laughter breaks out all around, the speaker gains confidence; he naturally gets carried away, doubles the truculence, rants on, falls into false fervor, into indignation, even into animosity, not existing in his heart; because, as I was in a position to know, the speaker would often happen to be one of the most accepting and humble human beings. In such cases, vainglory also comes into play and arouses the speaker, as does the desire to please each and every listener, a desire that at times compels the speaker to agree for appearances' sake with other people's ideas which he does not share in the least but with which he agrees in the hope that others will not jump on some sacred idea of his. Finally, conceit is also a factor since it arouses a person and compels him to demand the floor several times and to wait impatiently for the next gathering in order to refute his opponents—in a word, for many (for very many, in my sincere opinion) those evenings, those speeches and those conversations were pursuits taken as seriously as cards, chess-playing and so forth, irresistibly captivating in their own right, playing on a person's passions and appetites in exactly the same manner. A great number, in my opinion, deceived and ensnared themselves in that game at Petrashevsky's by taking what was a game for a serious enterprise. The same holds for the conversations which took place in small groups. All that was left unsaid, all the festering objections to some long speech that had to be listened to without interjecting a single comment, all this would pour forth at the end of the speech with a force proportional to the length of the speech, to the number in agreement with it and to the accumulation of internal contradictions within the speech. At such a time it is hard to refrain from making a truculent retort, from presenting a different view—one so imprudent and so out of character that it is quite likely that the person who makes such a comment will disavow it the day after or perhaps even right there an hour later because he has come to his senses, even if after the fact. In addition, the evenings spent at

Petrashevsky's were regarded as friendly get-togethers, as the gatherings of a circle of acquaintances and not at all as a club or a political group brought together by design.

I say this definitively, reasoning in the following way: that if (speaking hypothetically) there had indeed been someone who wanted to take part in a political meeting, in a secret society, in a club, then most likely he would not have mistaken for such a society the evenings at Petrashevsky's, at which there was nothing but chatter, chatter sometimes truculent in nature since the host vouched for the fact that the talk was among friends and even *en famille*, at which there was nothing but one little bell which was rung to demand the floor. But solely because of the fact that the gatherings were of a *friendly, familial* nature, if I may so express myself, solely for this reason, some people let down their guard and spoke carelessly. They spoke as they would never conceive of speaking in public. Who would not be found guilty if each were to be judged on the basis of his most secret thoughts and even on the basis of what he said in a close, tight, friendly circle, all but in private? But the domestic and the public man are different people. I was considerably surprised when at my first interrogation the Imperially-Established Commission submitted for my comment a remark pronounced by Durov, the purport of which was that "literature must be used to show the bureaucrats the very root of evil, in other words, the imperial authority." I know Durov personally. I remember well how he supported me warmly during my twice-told argument about literature with Petrashevsky, an argument in which I maintained that literature *has no need of orientation, aside from the strictly artistic*; consequently, literature has even less need of any orientation that would serve to make manifest— as it is put in the accusation, in the remark ascribed to Durov—the root of evil (there is no such need because such an orientation would be thrust upon the writer, hampering his liberty and what's more, it is a bilious, abusive orientation which would bring an end to artistic merit.*

The evening at which the discussion about bureaucrats took place, I was not at Petrashevsky's, as I have already had the honor of reporting; I heard about the argument the next day or the day after that (I do not remember exactly when) in a cursory fashion; I am not familiar with Durov's actual remarks. But being familiar with his way of thinking, I am convinced that these remarks were misunderstood by those who transmitted them, or else they were made in a fit, in a state of vexation caused by all the contentiousness, in the heat of the moment. I know Durov as the most mild-mannered man, yet at the same time he is pathologically irritable—to the point of having fits— and he is hot-tempered, he cannot refrain from speaking out, he forgets himself and sometimes will speak counter to his own heart-felt convictions, simply out of contrariness, when he is irritated with someone. Durov's close friends, Shchelkov and Palm know his unfortunate character even better than I and I am sure that they will corroborate what I say about him. What happened with Durov could have happened to a lesser or greater degree to anyone. I submit these observations and remarks of mine in the spirit of

justice, out of an innate sense, convinced that I have no right to hide them
them here as I make this response.

Fyodor Dostoevsky

*With which Petrashevsky was in complete agreement. It turned out that our argument had
been based on a misunderstanding. All Petrashevsky's guests were witnesses to this.

[Q:] Comment on the content of Timkovsky's speech at Petrashevsky's
and on the spirit in which it was given.

[A:] Timkovsky came to Petrashevsky's in the beginning of the winter,
he was there four or five evenings all told. He has one of those one-track
minds which once it latches on to some idea does so in such a way that this idea
prevails over all others, to their detriment. He was struck by the elegant
aspect of Fourier's system and he failed to notice other aspects which might
have cooled his excessive rapture for Fourier. What's more, he had only
recently familiarized himself with Fourier's system and had not had a chance
to turn it over in his mind in a critical fashion. This was apparent from
everything. And the fascination exerted by Fourier's system at first contact is a
known fact.

In all other respects, Timkovsky struck me as being a complete
conservative and by no means a freethinker. He is pious even about the
principles of autocracy. It is a known fact that Fourierism does not refute the
autocratic form of government. As for what concerns Timkovsky's personal
characteristics, apart from his political views, I can say this one thing: he
struck me as being very conceited.

As far as I can recall at this late date, his speech consisted of the
following:

First, he thanked everyone for giving him such a warm welcome, even
though three quarters of those in the room barely knew him by last name; that
is, his preamble was a bit bombastic and, indeed, the whole speech struck me
as being in the same vein. Then he announced that he was soon leaving
Petersburg and would be carrying away with him in his heart the consolation
of having been understood. Then he spoke about Fourier with great respect, as
I recall, he touched on the advantages of this system and expressed his desire
for its triumph. And yet Timkovsky recognized the impossibility of a speedy
application of the system. Then he called for agreement on certain principles
on the part of his listeners, no matter what social system they adhered to, but
he immediately made the proviso that he was neither calling for revolt nor
advocating a secret society; finally, he asked that our approval be expressed, if
he had earned it, by a handshake. The speech was written in a fiery tone; it was
apparent that Timkovsky had labored over the style and had tried to please all
tastes. But Timkovsky's orientation, in my opinion, was not a serious one. His
age notwithstanding, he is still in the first stage of his Fourierism, which he
happened to come across in the backwoods of provincial life. A lack of
external experience, an excess of inner passion, an inborn sensitivity for

elegance, which needs to be fed, and, most importantly, a lack of sound, serious education—all this, in my opinion, is what made him a Fourierist. At his age, everything takes somewhat deeper root than at first youth. In my view, he may renounce many of his Fourierist convictions so that of Fourier's system all that would remain would be what is useful in it. For his mind, thirsting after knowledge, needs to be fed continuously and education is the very best medicine against all delusion. This is my personal view of Timkovsky.

As for the impression he made at Petrashevsky's, well, it struck me as being quite ambivalent. Some regarded Timkovsky with derisive curiosity; out of scepticism, some doubted his sincerity. Some took him for a true, daguerrotypically faithful likeness of Don Quixote and perhaps they were not mistaken. In any event, everybody treated him most civilly and cordially.

Fyodor Dostoevsky

[Q:] Did you go to meetings at Speshnev's, Kashkin's, Kuzmin's, Durov's, Danilevsky's and were similar meetings also held elsewhere?

[A:] Speshnev was a personal acquaintance of mine, I would go to this house but I did not attend meetings there and nearly every time I went I found him home alone.

With Mssrs. Kashkin and Kuzmin I am not acquainted at all.

I saw Danilevsky last year two or three times at various people's houses. We were distantly acquainted; but I did not go to any evening gatherings at his house; furthermore, I have not seen him at all since May of 1848, except for a minute after his return and even then I did not have a chance to exchange a few words with him.

I did not go to any evening gatherings at Durov's.

My acquaintance with Durov and Palm began last winter. We were drawn together by a similarity of ideas and taste; both of them, Durov and especially Palm, made a most pleasant impression one me. Not having a large network of acquaintances, I prized these new acquaintances and did not want to lose them. Durov's circle of acquaintances came together on strictly artistic and literary ground. Soon we, that is, I, my brother, Durov, Palm and Pleshcheev, decided to publish a literary anthology and this is why we started getting together more often.[18] My brother wrote the prospectus for our publication; we began to discuss editorial matters. Since we wanted to edit the publication jointly, since we had to deliberate about the artistic merit of novels and stories intended for publication, the need naturally arose for us to reach a consensus on our literary ideas and to agree definitively on certain points regarding the publication about which there was still no agreement. We would see each other most often at Durov's apartment where we were most comfortable; the rest of us were somewhat constrained at home, my brother because of his family, Pleshcheev and I because of cramped quarters, and, consequently, we could not take turns being host. Our get-togethers soon turned into literary evenings at which there was also some music. Durov invited his closest acquaintances and the rest of us brought ours as well.

Eventually these get-togethers began to repeat themselves every week, most often taking place on Saturday. However, there was no fixed day.

Those evenings remained strictly literary and musical, in nature they were friendly and tightly-knit, since we had all managed to get to know each other rather well and things carried on in this same vein until an unfortunate proposal changed the tenor of those get-togethers in a flash.

It was suggested that our get-togethers were fruitless even to ourselves; that many of us were more specialized than the others in various fields of knowledge and various disciplines; that each had his own mind, his own viewpoint, his own observations and that if we were to share with each other our observations and knowledge then all would stand to benefit. This idea might have been met with sympathy had Filippov, the first to express it, not added onto it another proposal that completely changed its tenor and cast a particularly disturbing shadow on our get-togethers. Namely: he took it into his head to propose that we lithograph works which could be written by some member of our circle, bypassing the censorship.

[Q:] Who attended those meetings and what were they concerned with?

[A:] I became acquainted with Filippov last summer in Pargolovo.[19] He is still quite a young man, of a fiery nature and extremely inexperienced; he is game for any kind of wild behavior and thinks better of it only when it has led to trouble. But he has very many good qualities, for which I grew fond of him; namely—honesty, elegant manners, truthfulness, fearlessness and straightforwardness. He has yet another excellent quality which caught my attention: he follows other people's advice, whoever they may be, once he recognizes that they are right and he is immediately ready to admit his mistake and repent for it once others convince him that he is made one. But his fiery temperament and above all his early youth often get the better of his reason; in addition, he has another unfortunate quality, namely, conceit or, more accurately, vainglory, which in him reaches an absurd degree. He sometimes behaves as if he thought that everybody on earth doubted his courage and I think that he would go so far as to throw himself out of St. Isaac's Cathedral if somebody around whose opinion he valued happened to question whether or not he would have the courage to do it. I say this on the basis of fact. I was afraid of getting cholera in the first days of its outbreak. Nothing could have pleased Filippov more than to demonstrate to me throughout the livelong day that he was not in the least afraid of cholera. Simply for the sake of shocking me, he was not careful about his food, ate greens, drank milk and once when out of curiosity to see what would come of it I pointed out to him some rowanberries on a branch, which were completely green, having only just come out of the flower, and told him that I thought that if he ate those berries he would get cholera within five minutes, Filippov plucked off the whole cluster and ate half of it in front of my very eyes before I managed to stop him. This childish, foolhardy abandon, which deserves pity, unfortunately constitutes his main character trait. The very same conceit makes him exceedingly argumentative and he likes to argue about everything, whether he knows anything about it or not. In spite of his good education and his expertise in the field of physics and mathematics, a lack of real experience of life has kept him from developing serious views. Instead, his youth was lavishly endowed with all manner of distractions, often of a quite variegated and contradictory nature. Such is my impression of Filippov's character.

Almost everybody reacted quite negatively to his proposal. Everybody felt that things had gone too far and waited to hear what the others would have to say. I do not know, maybe I was mistaken but it seemed to me that half of those present did not speak out against Filippov simply because they were afraid that the other half would suspect them of cowardice and they also did not want to reject the proposal directly but rather by some round-about means. Furthermore, although we were all on rather close terms with each other, Durov's and Palm's older acquaintances had met their new ones, that is, us, only quite recently and they did not trust us completely. I forgot to say that Durov's and Palm's dearest and oldest acquaintances are Shchelkov, the Lamansky brothers and Kashevsky. Filippov had been brought into the group by me; I had invited Speshnev as well. Nevertheless, both Filippov and Speshnev had been already fairly well acquainted with Durov and Palm since they had had some contact with each other at Petrashevsky's. The discussion began; the drawbacks were presented; several sat silently, others talked, with Mombelli and Filippov doing most of the talking although I do not recall that Mombelli supported Filippov. Little by little, the friendly tone of our circle was spoiled. Durov walked to and from in the room and began to despair. I already had noticed that he was going to blow up. Kashevsky and Shchelkov, *totally indifferent to all that lay beyond the artistic activity of the circle*, took up their instruments in the hope of putting a stop to the matter. Some left early, immediately after supper. Eventually, Durov vented his vexation at Filippov by blowing up at him. He led him off into another room, seized on some remark of his and let loose a torrent of insults. Filippov behaved in a sensible fashion, he understood what was going on and did not respond in the heat of the moment. I went home earlier than usual that night.

The next day my brother informed me that he would not return to Durov's unless Filippov retracted his proposal and, as I recall, he also informed Filippov of the same thing when he saw him a few days later. I observed that several in the group felt the same way as my brother. At least, I know for a fact that Durov wanted to discontinue his evening gatherings as soon as possible. Finally, when we met the next time I asked that people hear me out and I dissuaded everyone by attempting to operate in my speech* by way of gentle mockery and at the same time sparing everyone's pride as much as possible. I succeeded and it seemed to me that this was what everybody had

---

*Actually, people did not make speeches at Durov's. I gave the first and last, it was the only one of them.

wanted to happen. Filippov's proposal was rejected then and there. Thereafter we met only once more. By then it was after Holy Week. During that period I was quite busy at home with my literary work and saw very few of my acquaintances and when I did it was on the run, but I do know that the evening gatherings ceased entirely because of Palm's illness.

This is all that I have to say about the meetings at Durov's.

Fyodor Dostoevsky

[Q:] You attended a luncheon at Speshnev's. Describe everything of consequence that took place at that luncheon.

[A:] At the luncheon at Speshnev's, Filippov's proposal was discussed. As it turned out, the morning was spent in a boring and inane fashion because of the friction which I sensed between Speshnev and Durov. As far as I know, this friction had arisen as a result of Filippov's proposal. Durov, who was angry with Filippov, had quarrelled with Mombelli and had announced that he did not want to have gatherings at his place and asked why others could not have them instead. Mombelli suggested that we meet at Speshnev's and Speshnev was coerced into hosting a morning gathering. Durov had said this because he wanted at all costs to be rid of Filippov's proposal and he was extremely irritable about everything. Speshnev let it be known to some of us in no uncertain terms that he'd been coerced into the luncheon and that it would be inconvenient for him to have us over again. We talked and nothing was resolved. Grigoriev read "Soldiers' Tale" but its author was not mentioned and I did not know who it was although I had my hunches. But, for that matter, I was not curious enough to find out who it was. It did not make a strong impression because everybody was distracted by various things and hardly anybody fancied such readings. We all parted company right after luncheon.

In my first deposition I passed over this luncheon in silence, first of all because it was a continuation of the same argument and secondly so as not to make public the unpleasant clash between Mombelli and Durov—similarly I did not testify about Grigoriev because I really do not know for sure who the author of "Soldiers' Tale" is.

Fyodor Dostoevsky

[Q:] It has been established that the following readings took place at the evening gatherings at Durov's:

Miliukov read his own translation from "Paroles d'un croyant," you read Belinsky's correspondence with Gogol, and Grigoriev read "Soldiers' Conversation." You are asked to comment on this.

[A:] Miliukov did in fact read his translation. He had previously let it be known that he had it; people asked him to bring it to read—out of curiosity.

On what day and in what month, I do not recall (it seems it was in March), I stopped by Durov's in the early afternoon and found Belinsky's correspondence with Gogol which had been sent to me. I read it on the spot to Durov and Palm. I was invited to stay to lunch. I stayed. Between five and six Petrashevsky dropped by and stayed for a quarter of an hour. He asked: "What is that notebook?" I told him that it was Belinsky's correspondence with Gogol and recklessly promised to read it at his house. When I did this I was acting under the influence of my first impression. Then, after Petrashevsky left, more people arrived and I stayed for tea. Of course, the conversation turned to the piece (of Belinsky's) and I read it again. But apart from Durov and Palm no more than six people heard it; that is all the guests there were. I remember that Mombelli, Lvov, the Lamansky brothers were there. Who else? I have forgotten. All this took place *on the very day* the article was received, when I was still under the influence of my *first* impression.

As regards Grigoriev's piece, "Soldiers' Conversation," I have already noted that it was read—neither at Durov's nor at an evening gathering, but at the luncheon at Speshnev's. The reading began so unexpectedly (that is, without preliminary explanation) that I did not even know who had written it or what was being read. I never discussed this piece with Grigoriev. It hardly made any impression. It is possible that someone sitting near Grigoriev made a few approbatory remarks simply to be polite. But I did not actually notice such a thing happening because I was sitting farther away from him than the others during the reading.

Fyodor Dostoevsky

[Q:] At the same evening gatherings Mombelli made a proposal to unite closely those attending so that under each other's influence they would strengthen their commitment and be more successful in promoting their ideas to the general public. Give commentary about this.

[A:] This occurred back when the evening gatherings at Durov's were first starting , it seems to me that it was at the very first one. Mombelli did in fact start to say something along those lines but I cannot recall all of what he said. But I do remember that he did not finish; because he was interrupted half way through and people started to play music. Mombelli began to laugh, he did not take offense at people's not paying attention and right away agreed that he had spoken inopportunely and no further mention was made about his remarks and our society remained strictly literary and musical for a long time.

Fyodor Dostoevsky

[Q:] At those same evening gatherings the student Filippov proposed undertaking a joint effort to produce articles in a liberal vein concerning issues related to the contemporary state of judicial and administrative affairs in Russia and print them on a private printing press. You are asked to comment on this.

[A:] It was not the student but the former student Pavel Filippov. As for what concerns the student Filippov, his brother, he was not acquainted with Durov, Petrashevsky or, it seems, any of us; I know him because I saw him three times or so when I went to see his brother, Pavel Filippov.

Pavel Filippov did make such a proposal. But in the question mention was made of *a private printing press*. I never heard anything said *about printing* at Durov's; or anywhere for that matter. No mention was made of this. What Filippov proposed was *lithography*. This is perfectly clear in my memory.

I have already given commentary about this proposal in one of the previous questions. This proposal came out of the blue, that is, in a society that was strictly literary and musical, and initially many were intrigued by its novelty. But, for that matter, I do not recall that Filippov uttered the words: *"in a liberal vein,"* rather, he simply invited people to engage in producing articles about Russia. At first some people responded positively to this proposal, strictly out of curiosity, but they pulled up short when it came to the subject of lithography. At that point, the great majority or perhaps even all of us (for what a person thinks privately to himself remains a mystery) were against this proposal. But talk about it continued for two more meetings (of which one was the luncheon at Speshnev's.) The talk seemed to drag on contrary to our wishes since everybody obviously wanted to distance themselves from it. But finally it was rejected and all declared themselves against it. About the manner in which it was rejected, I have already had the honor of giving commentary in one of the preceding questions.

Fyodor Dostoevsky

I recall that in the beginning, when there were as yet no evening gatherings at Durov's, when they were still in the planning stage and instituting them was still being discussed, Durov and I, as the first to decide upon these evenings, on several occasions reaffirmed the fact *that the evenings were to be established with a strictly literary and musical purpose, that there had not been, was not, and would not be any other clandestine, unspoken purpose to them.* Others were invited to these meetings openly, directly, without any form of enticement; no ulterior purpose was used as bait to lure anyone, and everyone was told (and even more than once) that *the society was strictly literary and musical and only literary and musical.*

Fyodor Dostoevsky

[Q:] At those same evening gatherings it was said that teachers in educational establishments ought to do their best to lecture in a liberal vein. Give commentary on this.

[A:] I have no recollection of this whatsoever.

Fyodor Dostoevsky

[Q:] If you know anything about any criminal conspiracy going on outside the meetings designated, you are obliged to give full and frank testimony about it here.

[A:] I have no knowledge of anything of the sort.

Fyodor Dostoevsky

[Q:] What do you know about the teacher Beletsky?
A:] I know nothing about the teacher Beletsky.

Fyodor Dostoevsky

[Q:] Comment on when and how a liberal or social orientation manifested itself in you.[20]

[A:] In all sincerity I say once again that my liberalism has consisted solely of my desire for all the best for my Fatherland, of my desire for its unceasing movement toward perfection. This desire dates from the point when I started to understand myself, it continued to grow in me but never crossed the boundary of the impossible. I have always believed in the government and autocracy. I dare not say that I have never been mistaken in my desires, that all of them have been right. It is possible that I have been very much mistaken in my desires for improvement and the common good, such that their fulfillment would have been to the general detriment rather than to the good. But I have consciously kept a watch over myself and quite often have modified my opinions. It is possible that I sometimes ended up expressing these opinions with excessive fervor or even bitterness; but that was momentary. *There has never been any malice or gall in me.* What is more, I have always been guided by the most *sincere* love for my Fatherland, a love which showed me the right path and (in this, I believe) kept me from erring grievously.

I desired many improvements and changes. I complained of many abuses. But my political thinking was grounded in the notion that these changes would come from the autocracy. All that I wanted was this—that nobody's voice be suppressed and that every need be heeded as much as possible. I know that the law protects each and every person; I believe in this, but there are violations and, unfortunately, many of them. And this is why I studied, why I thought things over on my own and why I enjoyed listening to conversation in which those who knew more than I spoke about the possibility of certain changes and improvements. But in me, I repeat, never did desire for the better exceed the realm of what is possible. As for my social orientation, I never was a socialist although I enjoyed reading about and studying social issues. First of all, socialism is the same old political economy, but cast in a different form. I enjoy studying matters of political economy. What is more, I am passionately fond of the historical sciences. This is why I followed the upheavals in the West with great interest. All this terrible drama concerned me deeply, first of all as a drama and secondly as an important event which at the very least was capable of evoking interest. Thirdly, as history, and, fourthly, in the name of love for my fellow man, because the present situation in the West is extremely disastrous. I occasionally spoke about political issues but seldom, hardly ever, out loud. I allowed the *historical necessity* of the current upheaval in the West, but—only pending improvement.

Socialism offers thousands of means for structuring society and since all those books are written cleverly, passionately and not infrequently with a genuine love for humanity, I read them with interest. But for the very reason that I do not subscribe to any social system and instead studied socialism as a general phenomenon, in all its systems, for this very reason I (although my knowledge is far from being definitive) see the shortcomings of each social system. I am convinced that the application of any one of them whatsoever would bring in its wake inescapable destruction. I am speaking not only about in this country but even in France. Such an opinion has been expressed by me time and time again. Finally, this is the conclusion I settled on. Socialism is a science in fermentation, it is chaos, it is alchemy rather than chemistry, astrology rather than astronomy; although, in my opinion, out of the present chaos something harmonious, practical and socially beneficial will subsequently develop, just as chemistry developed from alchemy and astronomy, from astrology.

Fyodor Dostoevsky

In all of these responses to the points of interrogation put to me I have written the absolute truth and have nothing to add, to which I put my signature

Retired Engineer-Lieutenant Dostoevsky

[Q:] Comment on when and how you became acquainted with Chernosvitov.

[A:] I first met Chernosvitov at Petrashevsky's, never having seen him before, and I have seen him no more than twice.

Fyodor Dostoevsky

[Q:] It has been established that at a meeting at Petrashevsky's Chernosvitov tried to promote the idea that liberalism and socialism are one and the same. Are you in a position to give substantive commentary on the content and orientation of this conversation?[21]

[A:] I did not catch the conversation about the identity of liberalism and socialism or Chernosvitov's opinion.

Fyodor Dostoevsky

[Q:] It has been established that at that same meeting at Petrashevsky's Chernosvitov tried when he spoke to provoke a truculent response from everyone and that, indeed, the conversation that evening was more truculent than ever before despite the fact that Lvov recited some fable. Are you in a position to give substantive commentary on this?

[A:] I did not notice any provocation of this sort; but he did speak boldly, sharply and his remarks often generated laughter. I definitely recall the fable being related.

Fyodor Dostoevsky

[Q:] It has been established that at that same meeting Chernosvitov made the following remark "And so our trouble, gentlemen, Russians' trouble is that we have gotten quite used to the stick—we think nothing of it"; to Speshnev's retort that it is a stick with two ends, Chernosvitov said "Yes, but we see only one of them."[22] Are you in a position to give substantive commentary on this subject?

[A:] I did not hear it said.

Fyodor Dostoevsky

[Q:] At that same meeting Chernosvitov said that Eastern Siberia was a separate country from Russia and was fated to be a separate empire, and he even invited everyone to go to Siberia, saying: "I tell you what, gentlemen, let's go to Siberia—it is a glorious country, they are a glorious people." Comment on the details and aim of this conversation.

[A:] I recall these remarks; but I do not remember the purport Chernosvitov gave them being such. He said that the Eastern region of Siberia indeed seemed to be like a separate country from Russia but, so far as I remember, in the climatic sense and because of the particular originality of its inhabitants. I definitely did not hear Chernosvitov express such an extreme view about Siberia being fated to be a separate empire and his remarks did not in my opinion have that purport.

Fyodor Dostoevsky

[Q:] Speaking about Chernosvitov as you were walking along with Speshnev you said: "The devil knows, this man speaks Russian exactly as Gogol writes it." After which, drawing up closer to Speshnev, you said: "Chernosvitov seems to me to be a spy." Comment on what in particular Chernosvitov said to instill in you the notion that he was a spy.

[A:] Nothing particular that he said but rather all of it instilled in me this idea which was, however, a momentary one. It struck me that there was something shifty in his conversation, as if, as they say, he *had something up his sleeve*. Since I only saw Chernosvitov once after that, I had even forgotten my remark until just now when I was asked to respond to the question.

Fyodor Dostoevsky

[Q:] Among your papers was found a note from Belinsky inviting you to a meeting at the home of somebody with whom you were not acquainted at the time. Comment on what kind of meeting it was, whether you attended and how many times.

[A:] I decidedly cannot recall anything about a note from Belinsky, I am not familiar with its contents and only now have learned for the first time that I had a note from Belinsky. But by such remarks I do not in any way wish to disavow my acquaintance with Belinsky. During the first year of our acquaintance, I was on rather close terms with him, in the second year, on rather distant terms and in the third year, he and I were at odds and I did not see him a single time.

If the note was an invitation then it most likely was written way back in the early days of our acquaintance and if he was inviting me to go somewhere then it would have been to pay a social call and not to attend any meeting. Belinsky's network of acquaintances, as far as I know, was very restricted and was limited to a small literary circle. He did not go to large meetings and could not bear them because he was unsociable, sickly and a homebody. He most likely wanted to introduce me to some literary person. Then, that is, in the early days of our acquaintance, he took great interest in me; for he had liked my first novel very much and he looked one me somewhat exaggerating my talent and significance. It was because of my novel that I was introduced to him. As I remember, we did not talk then about anything other than literature and for some months we carried on a heated argument about certain matters of a strictly literary nature. And so, I repeat, if I was invited to go somewhere, it was not to attend a meeting but to pay a social call on some litterateur. But where? how?—I cannot recall any of this because I have completely forgotten about the note and am not familiar with it. Nobody hosted any fixed meetings.

Fyodor Dostoevsky

[Q:] Among your books two banned ones were found: *Le Berger de Kravan* and *La Célébration du dimanche.* Explain from whom and by what means you acquired these books.

[A:] On the eve of my arrest, the 22nd of April, I stopped by Grigoriev's in the evening and took *Le Berger de Kravan* from his table. I did not have a chance to read even a single line from this book and therefore do not know what is in it. I took the other, *La Célébration du dimanche* from Golovinsky a week before my arrest, I think. I read just a few pages of it while still at Golovinsky's and since it seemed entertaining I took it with me. However, I cannot say whether Golovinsky knows of this because, as I recall, I forgot to ask his permission.

Fyodor Dostoevsky

[Q:] It has been established that you attended evening gatherings at Pleshcheev's at which somebody read a humorous piece entitled "Petersburg and Moscow," written by Herzen. State whether you attended these evening gatherings and comment on their orientation.

[A:] Pleshcheev never held any fixed evening gatherings. Only from time to time (although seldom) would he invite people over to tea. According to my recollection, it happened no more than three times during the winter. At those evening gatherings the talk was about everything in general and nothing in particular; that is, they were ordinary friendly gatherings, nothing more; and since there was no particular purpose to them, no particular orientation, everybody there acted just the same as they did at home or in any other place, there was nothing special. The guests were, to my knowledge, his close friends. That is all, according to my recollection. The piece "Petersburg and Moscow" was in fact read one time; but not at all out of subversive aims or with ulterior motive; rather, it was read casually, seemingly because it came to hand as a light satirical piece which contained a great deal of wit albeit along with a host of paradoxes; it was treated from a strictly literary standpoint. Such, at least, is my memory of it.

Fyodor Dostoevsky

[Q:] From the depositions of Speshnev and Danilevsky it is apparent that at Pleshcheev's evening gatherings there was discussion about the possibility of publishing banned books abroad. Give commentary about this.

[A:] At Pleshcheev's evening gatherings, about which I spoke in the preceding question, never was a single word uttered on such a subject. But I do recall that once, I forget precisely when, but a very long time ago, more than a year, I stopped by Pleshcheev's late at night, around eleven, and found Danilevsky and Speshnev there. And I remember that in fact a few remarks were made about the possibility of publishing abroad. At the time it seemed impossible for many reasons. Talk on this subject was not subsequently resumed and, in a word, it remained without consequences of any sort.

Fyodor Dostoevsky

Dostoevsky's Testimony from Related Cases

Testimony from the V. R. Zotov Case

[Q:] Respond: what are the name and patronymic of the literary gazette publisher, Zotov, what is his professional status, where is he employed, where does he live, and also what contact did he have with Petrashevsky, and what part did he take in the meetings when he was there?

[A:] His name, if I am not mistaken, is Vladimir Rafailovich. Where he is employed and lives, I do not know; for I never was personally acquainted with him. I did not know about his acquaintance with Petrashevsky and hear of it now for the first time. I never saw him at Petrashevsky's evening gatherings.

Fyodor Dostoevsky

[Q:] Do you know the name, patronymic and professional status of the literary gazette publisher, Mr. Zotov, and also where he is employed and where he makes his residence?

[Answer.] His name is Vladimir Rafailovich. I have no knowledge of his place of employment and residence.

Fyodor Dostoevsky

Testimony from the A. N. Maikov Case

[Q:] What is the patronymic of Valerian *Maikov*, who, according to your testimony, attended *Petrashevsky*'s meetings, and, also, what is his professional status, where does he work and where does he live?

Is he now deceased?

[A:] No doubt some mistake has been made in this question. I never testified a single word about Valerian Maikov or about his knowing Petrashevsky. My recollections on this score are accurate.

Valerian Nikolaevich Maikov died exactly two years ago on July 13, 1847. I was acquainted with him for only one year, on a literary basis. He had studied at the University, graduated and then taken a job—but where?—I cannot recall. I never saw him a single time at Petrashevsky's.* He knew Petrashevsky, but did not like either him or his meetings and tried to see him as seldom as possible. Twice I was witness to how he gave word that he was not at home when Petrashevsky came to call on him. He referred to him as a madman and I remember him saying that he would never go to Petrashevsky's on Fridays and that he did not like the company there at all.

This is all that I have to say about Valerian Nikolaevich Maikov.[23]

Fyodor Dostoevsky

Testimony from the A. P. Miliukov Case

[Q:] What role did Mr. Miliukov play in the meetings at Durov's and did he attend these meetings often?

[A:] At Durov's evening gatherings Mr. Miliukov was no different from any of the rest of the guests. Being himself a litterateur, his acquaintance with Durov and the company which gathered at Durov's was of a literary nature. Miliukov, it seemed to me, was universally liked for his cheerful, genial personality; moreover, he is a masterful joke-teller—such are his main characteristics. Once he happened to mention, I do not remember in what connection, that he had a rendition of Lamennais's famous piece in Slavonic. This seemed odd and curious and so he was asked to show it. Miliukov finally brought it and read it. When Filippov made his proposal, Miliukov, because of his vivacious nature, initially took part in the general discussion of it; but it struck me that he took fright at the second proposal: about the lithography. I arrive at this conclusion based on two recollections. First of all, the fact that he completely ceased talking about it whereas the discussion continued and that he did not even show up at Durov's for one of those evenings; nor did he go to the luncheon at Speshnev's, although he was invited. This last circumstance sticks in my memory because I remember everybody asking "where is Miliukov and why hasn't he come?" Secondly, the fact that I heard, and apparently from trustworthy sources, how Miliukov himself had said that he would break with Filippov's proposal and that he did not like it. All this happened even before my proposal (against Filippov.) I think that Miliukov even wanted to cease going to Durov's evening gatherings altogether. This was obvious from everything and mainly from the fact that he had stopped showing up of late. But here we have been arrested and I have not been able to verify my observations.

Fyodor Dostoevsky

[Q:] What part did did Mr. Miliukov play at the meetings at Durov's and Pleshcheev's?

---

*Except for one time, on Petrashevsky's name-day, when he was an invited quest.

[A:] At the meetings at Pleshcheev's, Miliukov did not distinguish himself in any particular fashion apart from the fact that he is a cheerful person, tells a good story and is a good listener. At Durov's, as has been established, he read his translation of Lamennais.

Fyodor Dostoevsky

Testimony from the N. A. Mordvinov Case

[Q:] Comment on the role played by Nikolai Mordvinov at the meetings at Pleshcheev's.

[A:] Nikolai Mordvinov, according to my knowledge, is an old acquaintance of Pleshcheev's and was a classmate of his at the university; he would come to Pleshcheev's as a close acquaintance. But he was always quiet. I did not notice anything particular about him.

Fyodor Dostoevsky

Testimony from the Cases of Romashov, Saltykov, Berdiaev, Yashvili, and the Cabbies, Fedotia and Mikhail Yakovlevy and Blium

[Q:] At what point did the titular counsellor Mikhail Saltykov start to attend the meetings at Petrashevsky's, when did he cease attendance of those meetings and what part did he take in them?

[A:] I do not recall that I ever met Mr. Saltykov at Petrashevsky's. Being only very slightly acquainted with Mr. Saltykov, I do not know anything about his relations with Petrashevsky. Nor did I ever heard a word about Mr. Saltykov from Petrashevsky.

Fyodor Dostoevsky

[Q:] Do you have any knowledge of what Petrashevsky's relations were with Yashvili, who took part in the conspiracy at Kiev University, or of where he is now and of what his professional status is?

[A:] I do not know anything at all about Mr. Yashvili, this is the first I have heard of him and likewise about the conspiracy that took place in the Kiev province. I do not know anything about Petrashevsky's relations with him.

Fyodor Dostoevsky

Testimony from the Cases of Implicated Persons

[Q:] Did Messrs. Bezobrazov and Palchikov attend the meetings at Pleshcheev's often and how did they participate in them?

[A:] I never once saw Mr. Palchikov at Pleshcheev's. Mr. Bezobrazov was there one time. He stayed about a half hour and participated in the same way as everyone else who had been invited to tea. He did not jump to my attention for any reason and consequently I have nothing special to say about him.

Fyodor Dostoevsky

[Q:] What are the name and patronymic of Mr. Vitkovsky who attended the meetings at Petrashevsky's, what is his professional status, where is he employed and where does he make his residence, and also do you know when he started attending these meetings and when his attendance ceased?

[A:] I never knew Mr. Vitkovsky, never heard about him and am now hearing of him for the first time. For this reason I cannot say whether he was at Petrashevsky's. I recall that I said in one of my responses that there were some people who went to Petrashevsky's I did not know at all, so that I was not even aware of their last names. Perhaps Mr. Vitkovsky belongs to this group of people? However, I repeat that I do not know anything at all about Mr. Vitkovsky.

Fyodor Dosotevsky

[Q:] What rank does Vladimir Kaidanov hold, where is he employed and and where does he make his residence; and also did he often attend the meetings at Petrashevsky's and Durov's and how did he take part in these meetings?

[A:] I know a Mr. Kaidanov whom I would see at Petrashevsky's, but I do not know his first name, nor do I know his rank and place of his employment. He, I believe, had been a schoolmate of Petrashevsky's at the Lyceum and they knew each other on this basis. He was not at Petrashevsky's often, to say that he came once a month would be an exaggeration; this, at least, is what I recall. He never took part in the general discussion and always sat off in another room with a book or with one of his acquaintances when people were talking in the main room. He was never at a single evening gathering at Durov's and I do not think that they were acquainted at all.

Fyodor Dostoevsky

[Q:] State how often and starting when the persons named below attended the meetings at Petrashevsky's; also their given names, patronymics and professional status, where they are employed and where they make their residence. Vernadsky.

[A:] I never heard this name mentioned at Petrashevsky's and never saw Mr. Vernadsky there.

[Q:] Avdeev.

[A:]I do not know such a person at all; I also do not know whether he was acquainted with Petrashevsky.

[Q:] Stalnitsky.

[A:] I know neither Mr. Stalnitsky nor whether he was acquainted with Petrashevsky.

[Q:] Grigoriev.

[A:] I cannot recall his name and patronymic. Nor his rank. It seems to me that he serves in the Life Guards of the Dragoon Regiment. He has been acquainted with Petrashevsky, as I recall, since January of 1849. He lives on Gorokhovaya Street, near the Semenovsky Bridge, in Sebastyanov's building.

[Q:] Ratovsky.

[A:] I do not know anything about Mr. Ratovsky or about whether he was acquainted with Petrashevsky.

[Q:] Stepanov.

[A:] I never knew Mr. Stepanov nor whether he is acquainted with Petrashevsky.

[Q:] Aslan.

[A:] I do not know Mr. Aslan. I do not know whether he was acquainted with Petrashevsky.

[Q:] Grenkov.

[A:] I do not know Mr. Grenkov. I do not know whether he was acquainted with Petrashevsky.

[Q:] Poliansky.

[A:] I do not know Mr. Polyansky. I do not know whether he was acquainted with Petrashevsky.

[Q:] Motrashenko.

[A:] I do not know Mr. Motrashenko. I do not know whether he was acquainted with Petrashevsky.

[Q:] Mikhailov.

[A:] I know Mr. Mikhailov only by his last name; I recall neither his rank nor his name. I know nothing about when he and Petrashevsky became acquainted but I seem to have seen him at Petrashevsky's once last year. However, I do not recall for sure. I do not know where he lives.

[Q:] Makeev.

[A:] I do not know Mr. Makeev. I do not know whether he was acquainted with Petrashevsky.

[Q:] Stasov (1).

[A:] I never heard about an acquaintance between Mr. Stasov (1) and Petrashevsky and I never saw him at Petrashevsky's. I know neither his rank, nor his given name nor his place of residence.

[Q:] Stasov (2).

[A:] I never heard about an acquaintance between Mr. Stasov (2) and Petrashevsky and I never saw him at Petrashevsky's. I know neither his rank, nor his given name nor his place of residence.

[Q:] Sipko.

[A:] I do not know Mr. Sipko; I do not know whether he was acquainted with Petrashevsky.

[Q:] Sundukov (1).

[A:] I do not know Mr. Sundukov (1). I do not know whether he was acquainted with Petrashevsky.

[Q:] Sundukov (2).

[A:] I do not know Mr. Sundukov (2). I do not know whether he was acquainted with Petrashevsky.

[Q:] Nazarov.

[A:] I do not know Mr. Nazarov. I do not know whether he was acquainted with Petrashevsky.

[Q:] Petrov.

[A:] I do not know Mr. Petrov. I do not know whether he was acquainted with Petrashevsky.

[Q:] Vzmetnev.

[A:] I do not know Mr. Vzmetnev. I do not know whether he was acquainted with Petrashevsky.

[Q:] Burnashev.

[A:] I do not know Mr. Burnashev. I do not know whether he was acquainted with Petrashevsky.

[Q:] Pyotr Petrovich Semyonov.

[A:] I do not know Mr. Semyonov. I do not know whether he was acquainted with Petrashevsky.

[Q:] Lukin (the teacher), Vasily Vasilevich.

[A:] I do not know Mr. Lukin. I do not know whether he was acquainted with Petrashevsky.

Fyodor Dostoevsky

F. M. Dostoevsky's Signed Statement for the Military-Judicial Commission

To the retired engineer-lieutenant Dostoevsky.

The Military-Judicial Commission imperially-established to judge you according to the military field laws submits the following for your response: do you have, in addition to the testimony already given by you under investigation, anything further to present in your defense?

I have nothing new to present in my defense with the possible exception of the fact that I never acted with malice or premeditation against the government. What I did do was done thoughtlessly on my part and much of it all but unintentionally, such as, for example, the reading of Belinsky's letter. If ever I spoke freely, then it was only among a circle of friends who were in a position to understand me and knew the purport of what I said. But I always refrained from disseminating my misgivings.

Fyodor Dostoevsky
October 20th, 1849

The Third Department's Secret Orders for Dostoevsky's Arrest

Secret.

The Third Department of His Imperial Majesty's Own Chancellery, First Section. Saint Petersburg. April 22, 1849. No. 675.

To the Major of the Saint Petersburg Gendarme District, Mr. Chudinov.

By imperial command, I order your Honor to arrest tomorrow at 4 o'clock in the morning the retired engineer-lieutenant and litterateur, Fyodor Mikhailovich Dostoevsky, who lives at the corner of Malaia Morskaia Street and Voznesensky Prospect, in Shil's building, on the third floor, in Bremer's apartment, and to seal up his papers and books and to deliver the above-mentioned, along with Dostoevsky, to the Third Department of His Imperial Majesty's Own Chancellery.

At which occasion you must keep a vigilant watch to insure that none of Dostoevsky's papers be concealed.

It may so happen that you will find in Dostoevsky's possession a great quantity of papers and books such that it will be impossible to deliver them all at once to the Third Department; if such is the case, you must place both the papers and the books in one or two rooms, as necessity dictates, and then seal off these rooms and present Dostoevsky himself to the Third Department forthwith.

If, when his papers are sealed, Dostoevsky should specify that some of the aforementioned belong to other persons, these specifications are to be ignored and the aforementioned are to be likewise sealed up.

In the execution of this assignment entrusted to you, you must exercise supreme caution, for which you will be held personally accountable.

The Chief of Staff of the Corps of Gendarmes, General-Lieutenant Dubelt will make arrangements for you to be accompanied by an officer of the St. Petersburg police and the required number of gendarmes.

General-Aide de Camp Count Orlov

Excerpt from the "Record of Persons Attending Petrashevsky's Friday Meetings from March 11th of this Year" [1849]

Top Secret.

Name, Professional Status and Place of Employmment
Dostoevsky, first, Fyodor Mikhailov: retired engineer-litterateur.
One of the most important.

Residence
1st section, 2nd block on the corner of Malaya Morskaya and Voznesensky Prospect in Shil's building, on the third floor, in Bremer's apartment.

Comment
On March 11th and 25th and on April 1st he was at the meetings and on the 1st of April took part in debate on three issues: freedom of the press, the emancipation of the serfs and the reform of the judicial system, agreeing with Golovinsky's opinion. [...] On April 15th he was at the meeting and read Belinsky's letter in answer to Gogol at the session. This letter contains the most impertinent and criminal expressions, etc. It is the property of Filippov. [...] According to what Petrashevsky says, the Dostoevsky brothers and the Maikov brothers play the principal role in a society made up of litterateurs.

Memorandum of the Chairman of the Commission for the Examination of the Prisoners' Papers to the Chairman of the Secret Investigatory Commission.

May 16th, 1849   Copy

Secret

Ivan Alexandrovich, sir,

Upon examination of the papers of Lieutenant *Dostoevsky* nothing was found that relates directly to the immediate case, but the following were found: a note to him from *Belinsky*, containing an invitation to a meeting in the home of someone with whom he was not yet acquainted, and a letter from Moscow, written by *Pleshcheev* in which he refers to the impression made by the Imperial family's stay in Moscow and in which he instructs Dostoevsky to convey his respect to persons implicated in the society in question. These papers and two banned books entitled: 1. *Le Berger de Kravan* and 2. *La Célébration du dimanche*—I have the honor of forwarding to your Excellency herewith, most humbling beseeching you to accept assurance of my full respect and devotion.

Signed: Prince Alexander Golitsyn
Verified: State Councillor Shmakov

No. 49
May 16th 1849
to his Excellency I. A. Nabokov

Antonelli's Report

Dostoevsky (1), according to Antonelli's reports, was at the meetings at Petrashevsky's on March 11th, 18th and 25th and on April 1st and 15th.[24]

At the meeting on March 11th [...] Toll gave a speech about the origins of religion and explored the question of whether or not there exists in people a religious feeling, arguing that religion is not only not necessary socially but even harmful because it hinders the development of the mind, etc. Toll's speech met with general approval.

At the meeting on March 18th [...] Yastrzhembsky gave a speech about the sciences, explaining that all sciences and particularly statistics, directly point to a social form of government as being the best. In his speech Yastrzhembsky often referred to Proudhon and spoke out not only against high officials but even against the Emperor.

At the meeting on March 25th [...] of March, the manner in which the the subjects should be set against the authorities was discussed. Durov argued that each person should be shown evil at its very source, that is, in the law and ruler and that the subjugated people should be incited not against their superiors but against the very source of evil. Balasoglo, Berestov, Filippov, Kaidanov and someone else objected that, on the contrary, the subjugated people should be incited against the most immediate authorities and, passing from the lower to the higher, unwittingly, gropingly, be led to the very source of evil. Upon which Filippov said: "Our system of propaganda is the best and to renounce it would mean renouncing the possibility of realizing our ideas." Whereupon Toll read a piece about the origins of religion written by him in the same vein as before; and Balasoglo read the foreword to the works of Khmelnitsky, written by Durov and containing many liberal ideas; at which point Petrashevsky, thanking the author, added that all must strive to write in a similar vein because although the censors would expunge ten, even twenty thoughts and ideas, five would yet remain.

At the meeting on April 1st [...] the talk was about the freedom of the press, change in the judicial system and the emancipation of the peasants. Golovinsky argued that the emancipation of the peasants should come first; whereas Petrashevsky maintained that attaining improvements in the judicial system was much surer and safer. In the midst of this discussion,

Golovinsky said that a change of government could not occur suddenly and that, to begin with, a dictatorship must be established. Petrashevsky strongly objected to this and said in conclusion that he would be first to raise his hand against the dictator. Mombelli said that if it were impossible presently to think about the emancipation of the serfs then at least each landholder should make it his sacred duty to concern himself with the education of the peasants, with establishing schools among them and with instilling in them a sense of their own self-worth. The *whole meeting* agreed with Mombelli's opinion with the exception of Grigoriev.

At the meeting on April 15th [...] *Dostoevsky* read Gogol's correspondence with Belinsky and in particular Belinsky's letter to Gogol. In this letter Belinsky, examining the plight of Russia and its populace, spoke first of the Orthodox religion in unseemly and impertinent terms and then about the judicial system, laws and the authorities. This letter evoked a great deal of enthusiasm and approval from the group, particularly from Balasoglo and Yastrzhembsky, principally in the passage where Belinsky says that the Russian people does not have a religion. It was decided to circulate this letter in several copies. At which point Petrashevsky said that an insurrection must not be undertaken without certainty of complete success and he set forth his view on how to achieve such a goal. After this, discussion returned to the three main issues examined on April 1st; the speakers were Petrashevsky, Akhsharumov and Golovinsky; the latter more than the others explored this subject, promising to develop the aforementioned fully on the following two Fridays.

Yastrzhembsky, who also took part in the conversation, offered to develop this subject from his own point of view.

Note 1. Petrashevsky, as Antonelli reports, said that on Friday (March 4th) among those at his house were the *Dostoevsky* brothers with whom Petrashevsky quarrelled, criticizing them for their manner of writing which appeared not to promote any kind of development of ideas in the public.

Note 2. Antonelli reports that Petrashevsky mentioned that some society exists, comprised of litterateurs, in which the Maikov brothers and the *Dostoevsky* brothers play the leading role.

The Testimony of Dostoevsky's Co-Defendants

Akhsharumov, Timkovsky, Yastrzhembsky and Filippov testified: that *Dostoevsky* read the manuscript "Gogol's Correspondence with Belinsky" at a meeting at Petrashevsky's, that Filippov had made a copy from the manuscript of Dostoevsky, who subsequently kept both for himself; he had received it from Moscow, apparently from Pleshcheev. To this Filippov added that Dostoevsky read "Gogol's Correspondence with Belinsky" another time, at an evening gathering at Durov's.

From the testimony of Speshnev, Mombelli and Akhsharumov it has been established that *Dostoevsky* was also present at the evening gathering at Petrashevsky's (in December of the past year, 1848) at which Timkovsky gave a speech about socialism.

In this speech (according to Mombelli's testimony) Timkovsky discussed progress, Fourierism, communism and propaganda, then he suggested dividing the world into two parts, rendering one part as a testing ground to the Fourierists and the other to the communists and he finished with the suggestion that discussion circles be organized which would concern themselves exclusively with issues related to communism, the participants of these circles gathering in their circle for the debate of controversial and particularly troublesome issues. Timkovsky's speech made a most grim impression.

In the papers of Dostoevsky, according to the information from the Secretary of State, Prince Golytsyn, nothing was found directly related to the case, but the following items were found: a note to him from Belinsky containing an invitation to a meeting in the home of a person with whom he was not yet acquainted and a letter from Moscow from *Pleshcheev* in which he refers to the impression made by the Imperial family's stay in Moscow, in the following terms:

"The Tsar and the Court meet with very little sympathy here. All, with the possible exception of those belonging to the Court,—want them to leave as soon as possible. Even the populace somehow does not express particular sympathy" etc.

Within this same letter, Pleshcheev instructs Dostoevsky to convey his respects to all who attended the Saturdays at the homes of Durov, Palm and Shchelkov, and to the three of them in particular.

Summary of the Defendants' Testimony

Dostoevsky testified that he has never been on very close terms with Petrashevsky although he did attend his Friday gatherings, just as Petrashevsky in turn would call on him. It was the type of acquaintance which he did not prize very highly since he and Petrashevsky lacked common ground both in their personalities and in many of their views, and visiting Petrashevsky very rarely, he maintained relations with him only to the extent required by courtesy, he had no reason to break off relations with him entirely, besides which it was sometimes interesting for him to attend Petrashevsky's Friday gatherings not so much for Petrashevsky's sake as for the sake of seeing certain people whom he saw only extremely rarely and whom he liked.

During last winter, from September on, he, *Dostoevsky*, was not at Petrashevsky's more than eight times. He has always been struck by the peculiarity of Petrashevsky's behavior and he, Dostoevsky, heard it said several times that Petrashevsky has more brains than sense. He is a man who is forever fussing about something, he reads a lot, he admires Fourier's system which he has studied in detail and, in addition, he is very involved in studying law. But, in any event, he, Dostoevsky, always respected Petrashevsky as an honest and noble man. It would be hard to say whether Petrashevsky regarded as a political figure has any particular ideological system of his own or some particular point of view on political events. As far as he, Dostoevsky, could tell, his views were consistent only in regard to Fourier's system, and that was actually, he thought, what kept him from looking at things in an original way. Yet he, Dostoevsky, can quite definitely say that Petrashevsky is quite far from believing in the possibility of an immediate application of Fourier's system to our social reality.

According to him, *Dostoevsky*, the group that gathered at Petrashevsky's on Fridays consisted almost entirely of his close friends and old acquaintances; sometimes new faces would appear but as far as he could tell this happened rather rarely. In Petrashevsky's group, he, Dostoevsky, met with no unity whatsoever, no orientation, no common cause and he can positively say that three among them could not be found who would all agree to some point on any given subject. From this resulted the arguments among one another, the endless contradictions and differences of opinion; in a few of these arguments he, Dostoevsky, himself took part. He spoke at Petrashevsky's three times: twice about literature and once about a subject that was completely non-political: about individuality and human egoism and he does not recall that there was anything political or freethinking about what he said. If seeking the better is liberalism, then, in this sense he, Dostoevsky, may be a freethinker, as would be any man who feels that he has the right to be a citizen and to seek the welfare of his country because in his heart he finds both love for his country and the knowledge that he has never in any way done it harm.

"If the charges against me are," explains Dostoevsky, "that I spoke about politics, the West, censorship and so on, then who in our day has not spoken and thought about these issues? Why was I educated, why has a desire for knowledge been aroused in me by learning if I do not have the right to voice my personal opinion or disagree with that opinion which retains its authority no matter what? One must not conclude from this that I am a freethinker and opponent of the autocracy, on the contrary, for me there never was anything more absurd than the idea of republican rule in Russia, and my ideas on this are familiar to all who know me. Speaking about censorship, about its inordinate severity in our time, I lamented this fact, for I felt that some misunderstanding had taken place, resulting in a strained state of affairs that was hard on literature. It saddened me that in our day the calling of the writer has been debased by some dark suspicion and that, from the outset, even before he has written anything, the writer is regarded by the censors as if he were some natural enemy of the state and they set to picking apart his manuscripts with unmistakable prejudice."

He, Dostoevsky, read the article "Belinsky's Correspondence with Gogol" at one of the evening gatherings at Petrashevsky's, but in doing so there was nothing in his judgments or even in the intonation of his voice or in his posture during the reading that was capable of signalling his partiality for either of the correspondents. Belinsky's letter is written in too strange a way to evoke a sympathetic response; it is filled with rebukes, written with gall and for this reason repels the heart. He, Dostoevsky, was on rather close terms with Belinsky and thus the latter's correspondence with Gogol was for him a rather remarkable literary monument. As for him, Dostoevsky, he was literally not in agreement with a single of the exaggerations found in the article and would never have gotten it into his head to read it presenting it as a model that ought to be followed; only now has he realized that he made a mistake and ought not to have read the article out loud.

As for the question as to whether the Petrashevsky group had some hidden, clandestine purpose, bearing in mind all the confusion of ideas and personalities in Petrashevsky's group and of arguments, going to the brink of hostility, it can definitely be said that it would have been out of the quesiton for there to have been such a purpose in all that chaos.

In conclusion, Dostoevsky added that he cannot say anything at all about Petrashevsky as a Fourierist propagator and that he is familiar in this regard only with his scholarly views; Petrashevsky never imparted to him any plans or instructions and he, Dostoevsky, definitely does not know whether he had any or not.

Excerpt from the Case of the
Retired Engineer-Lieutenant Fyodor Dostoevsky

According to the agent's reports, Dostoevsky is guilty of having been at the evening gatherings at the titular counsellor Butashevich-Petrashevsky's on April 1st and 15th of the current year, 1849, at which there was discussion about freedom of the press, change in the judicial system and the emancipation of the peasants and at which was read by him, Dostoevsky, Gogol's correspondence with Belinsky of which the latter's letter to Gogol is filled with impertinent freethinking.

The following testimony was given by other defendants:

Mombelli and Akhsharumov testified that Dostoevsky was at the evening gathering at Petrashevsky's (in December of 1848) when Timkovsky gave a speech in which (as Mombelli testifies) Timkovsky discussed progress, Fourierism, communism and propaganda; then he suggested dividing the world into two parts, rendering one part as a testing ground to the Fourierists and the other to the communists and he finished with the suggestion that discussion circles be organized which would concern themselves exclusively with issues related to communism, the participants of these circles gathering in their circle for the debate of controversial and particularly troublesome issues. Timkovsky's speech made a most grim impression.

The student Filippov testified that Dostoevsky among others attended evening gatherings at Durov's at which the talk began from March, 1849, to take on a political nature, starting with Mombelli's presenting an argument to the effect that they all, being more or less of the same orientation and ideological outlook, must unite closely among themselves so that under each other's influence they would fortify their commitment and orientation and be more successful in promoting their ideas to the general public, and with Filippov's own proposal to undertake a joint effort to produce articles in a liberal vein, regarding it as their duty to disseminate their opinions and to unmask all the legal injustices, all the abuses and shortcomings in the organization of our administration. When the next time at Durov's, he, Filippov, read a manuscript from the "Sayings of a Believer" of Lamennais[25] and Dostoevsky read Gogol's correspondence with Gogol and those present expressed a desire to have copies of this manuscript it was proposed that they establish a private lithography, but Dostoevsky convinced everyone that the idea was foolhardy. In addition, somebody at Durov's said that teachers in educational establishments ought to do their best to lecture in a liberal vein.

The landowner Speshnev testified that at a luncheon at his house when Grigoriev read the article of criminal content under the title of "Soldiers' Conversation," Dostoevsky was among those present.

In addition, Speshnev gave evidence that Dostoevsky also attended evening gatherings at Pleshcheev's at which a humorous piece, entitled "Petersburg and Moscow," was read and the possibility of publishing banned books abroad was discussed.

Among Dostoevsky's papers were found: 1) a letter to him from Pleshcheev sent from Moscow in which Pleshcheev instructs Dostoevsky to convey his respects to all who attend the Saturday gatherings at the homes of Durov, Palm and Shchelkov and to the three of them in particular, and in which he refers to the impression made by the Imperial family's stay in Moscow in the following terms: "The Tsar and the Court meet with very little sympathy here. All, with the possible exception of those belonging to the Court, want them to leave as soon as possible. Even the populace somehow does not express particular sympathy" etc.; 2) a note from Belinsky containing an invitation for Dostoevsky to attend a meeting in the home of a person with whom he was not yet acquainted, and 3) two banned books, entitled "Le Berger de Kravan" and "La Célébration du dimanche."

Dostoevsky testified that he has been acquainted with Petrashevsky for three years and that at first he went to his house seldom but that during the past winter he started going more often and took part in the discussion and the arguments. If the charges against him are that he spoke about politics, about the West, about literature and so on, then who in our day has not spoken and thought about these issues? Why was he educated, why has a desire for knowledge been aroused in him by learning if he does not have the right to voice him personal opinion or disagree with the opinion that retains its authority no matter what? One must not conclude from this that he, Dostoevsky, is a freethinker and opponent of the autocracy—on the contrary, for him there never was anything more absurd than the idea of republican rule in Russia. Speaking about censorship, about its inordinate severity in our time, he, Dostoevsky, lamented this fact, for he felt that some misunderstanding had taken place, resulting in a strained state of affairs that was hard on literature. It saddened him that in our day the calling of the writer has been debased by some dark suspicion and that, from the outset, even before he has written anything, the writer is regarded by the censors as if he were some natural enemy of the state and they set to picking apart his manuscripts with unmistakable prejudice. However, he, Dostoevsky, never spoke about these things at Petrashevsky's and just felt like having a chance to express his train of thought. He read Belinsky's letter to Gogol at the meeting at Petrashevsky's as a literary monument which was remarkable to him, Dostoevsky, because of his close acquaintance with Belinsky; and having volunteered to do so upon seeing Petrashevsky at Durov's he could not then break his word. But he was firmly convinced that the letter, filled with rebukes, written with gall and for this reason repelling the heart, could not lead anyone into temptation. And yet he has now realized that he made a mistake when he read the article out loud, which he ought not to have done.

At the evening gatherings at Petrashevsky's, he, Dostoevsky, heard what Petrashevsky said about the service performed by the censorship in expunging all nonsense from works and about the fact that if censorship were to be done away with, throngs of people would appear on the scene, attracted by personal desires, who would stand in the way of human progress and of the achievement of goals dear to them all; he, Dostoevsky himself, argued that literature has no need of orientation other than the strictly artistic. Golovinsky spoke enthusiastically about how the overriding concern of each individual ought to be the emancipation of the peasants, of those oppressed, suffering victims; but that the government could not do it since they could not be emancipated without land and about how he, Golovinsky, acknowledged the possibility of a sudden insurrection, initiated by the peasants acting on their own, since their tribulation already weighs heavily upon their consciousness,—but that he expressed this as a fact rather than as something he hoped for, since in allowing for the possibility of the emancipation of the peasants he is far from revolt and from a revolutionary mode of activity. In refutation of Golovinsky, Petrashevsky explained that when the peasants were emancipated a clash between classes was bound to occur which, being disastrous in and of itself, might be even more disastrous since it would give rise to military despotism or, what's even worse, spiritual depotism; that judiciary reform and reform of the censorship were more immediately necessary than peasant reform and he even calculated the advantage the serf segment of the peasantry has over the free segment under our present judicial system, explaining that in our tangled, multifarious, biased judicial system justice cannot be effected and that there is only one conceivable judicial system in which its goal, that is, justice, can be effected and that is a public judicial system—trial by jury; but these changes in the judicial system ought not to be demanded but rather most humbly beseeched since the government, whether it refuses or fulfills the estate's request, will worsen its position: by refusing the request, it incites it against itself and our cause will gain ground; by fulfilling the request, it will weaken itself and allow the opportunity for making greater demands and all the same our cause gains ground.

About the speech made by Timkovsky at the meetings at Petrashevsky's, Dostoevsky testified that it was written in a fiery tone and that it was apparent that Timkovsky had tried to please all tastes. It took up two or three evening gatherings but he, Dostoevsky, was only there for two of those evenings. Timkovsky spoke about Fourier with great respect, touched on many of the advantages of his system and expressed his desire for its triumph although he was convinced of the impossibility of its immediate application; he called for agreement on certain principles on the part of his listeners, no matter what social system they adhered to, and at the same time made the proviso that he was neither calling for revolt nor advocating a secret society; finally he asked those present to express their approval if he had earned it. The impression made by Timkovsky was ambivalent: some regarded him with derisive curiosity, whereas others, sceptical, doubted his sincerity; in any event everybody treated him most civilly.

About the evening gatherings at Durov's, Dostoevsky testified that he attended them himself and brought Filippov and Speshnev into their midst. These evening gatherings were literary at first but then changed their tenor when Filippov made a proposal to lithograph works which could be written by some member of the circle, bypassing the censorship. But almost everybody reacted quite negatively to this proposal and everybody, realizing that they had gone too far, wanted to reject it, only not directly but rather by some round-about means; Durov himself wanted to discontinue his evening gatherings as soon as possible. Finally, when they met the next time, he, Dostoevsky, having asked that people hear him out, dissuaded everyone by attempting to operate in his speech by way of gentle mockery and everybody seemed to have been waiting for this to happen; Filippov's proposal was turned down then and there. Thereafter they gathered at Durov's only once more, after Holy Week, the evening gatherings then ceasing completely. Nobody other than Dostoevsky made speeches at those evening gatherings and he made only one speech, whereas the following readings took place: Miliukov read his translation of "Paroles d'un croyant"; and he, Dostoevsky, upon receiving Belinsky's correspondence with Gogol, read it first to Durov and Palm, before luncheon; and then, having stayed for tea, upon the arrival at Durov's of Mombelli, Lvov and the Lamansky brothers, he read it again, while under the influence of his first impression.

To the question about Mombelli's proposal to unite closely those attending so that under each other's influence they would stengthen their commitment and be more successful in promoting their ideas to the general public, Dostoevsky testified that when the evening gatherings at Durov's were beginning Mombelli did in fact start to say something along those lines but did not finish because he was interrupted half way through and people started to play music. Mombelli began to laugh and right away agreed that he had spoken inopportunely. Thereafter no further mention was made about his remarks and the society remained strictly literary and musical for a long time.

About the luncheon at Speshnev's, Dostoevsky testified that he was at that luncheon and heard Grigoriev's reading of the article of criminal content entitled "Soldiers' Conversation"; but that the impression it made was not very strong because hardly anybody fancied such readings, and Speshnev, who had been coerced into having the luncheon after Mombelli's suggestion, let it be known in no uncertain terms that it would be inconvenient for him to have them over again.

To the question about evening gatherings at Pleshcheev's, Dostoevsky testified that he never held any fixed evening gatherings and only from time to time would invite people over to tea. He, Dostoevsky, was at such evening gatherings no more than three times in the course of the winter and since they were ordinary friendly get-togethers and there was no particular purpose to them, they had no particular orientation. The piece "Petersburg and Moscow" was in fact read once, but not out of subversive aim or with ulterior motives, rather, it was read casually , seemingly because it came to hand as a light satirical piece which contained a great deal of wit albeit along with a host of paradoxes; it was treated from a strictly literary standpoint. Moreover, once, more than a year before, he, Dostoevsky, stopped by Pleshcheev's at eleven at night and found Danilevsky and Speshnev there. At that time a few remarks were in fact made about the possibility of publishing abroad but it seemed impossible to him, Dostoevsky, for many reasons and thereafter talk on this subject remained without consequences of any sort and was not subsequently resumed.

In regard to the note from Belinsky found among the papers in his, Dostoevsky's, possession, containing an invitation to a meeting in the home of somebody with whom he was not acquainted at the time, and to the two banned books—he, Dostoevsky, explained that he decidedly could not recall anything about the note but that it was most likely to have been written in the early days of his acquaintance with Belinsky, who if he was inviting him to go somewhere did not invite him to attend a meeting but to pay a social call on some litterateur. The banned books had been borrowed by him, Dostoevsky, one from Grigoriev and the other from Golovinsky.

To the question as to when and how a liberal or political orientation manifested itself in him, Dostoevsky, he testified that his liberalism consisted solely of his desire for all the best for his fatherland. This desire dates from the point when he started to understand himself and it continued to grow in him; but it never crossed the boundary of the impossible. He always believed in the government and autocracy; however he dares not say that he has never been mistaken in his desires, which in terms of their contribution to bringing about improvement and the common good might have been mistaken such that their fulfillment would have been to the general detriment rather than to the good. It is possible that he sometimes ended up expressing his opinions with excessive fervor or even bitterness but that was momentary. There was never any malice or gall in him and what's more he has always been guided by the most sincere love for his fatherland, a love which showed him the right path and protected him from fatal errors. He desired many improvements and changes and complained of many abuses; but his political thinking was grounded in the notion that these changes would come from the autocracy. He wanted for nobody's voice to be suppressed and for every need to be heeded as much as possible and for this reason studied, thought things over on his own and enjoyed listening to conversation in which those who knew more than he spoke about the possibility of certain changes and improvements. As for his social orientation, he was never a socialist although he enjoyed reading about and studying social issues and followed the upheavals in the West with great interest. All this terrible drama concerned him deeply, first of all as a drama; second, as an important event which was capable of evoking interest, third, as history and fourth, in the name of love for his fellow man; for the present situation in the West is extremely disastrous. He occasionally spoke about political issues but seldom or hardly ever out loud and he allowed the historical necessity of the current upheaval in the West until improvements occur. Socialism offers thousands of means for structuring society and since all the (social) books are written cleverly, passionately and not infrequently with a genuine love for humanity, he, Dostoevsky, read them with interest; but this does not mean that he subscribes to any social system, being convinced that their application not only in Russia but even in France would bring in its wake inescapable destruction.

Dostoevsky, according to his testimony, is twenty-seven years old; he was educated at the Central Engineering Institute at personal expense; in 1843 he enrolled in service at the drafting office of the Engineering Department; in 1844 he retired with the rank of lieutenant.

Councillor of State Shmakov

The Sentence of the Military-Judicial Commission

The Military Court finds the defendant Dostoevsky guilty of, upon receiving in March of this year from Moscow, from the nobleman Pleshcheev (a defendant), a copy of a criminal letter by Belinsky, having read this letter at meetings: first, at the home of the defendant Durov and then at the home of the defendant Petrashevsky, eventually giving it to the defendant Mombelli to be copied.[26] Dostoevsky was at the home of the defendant Speshnev when the subversive work by the lieutenant Grigoriev entitled "Soldiers' Conversation" was read. Hence the Military Court has sentenced him, the retired engineer-lieutenant Dostoevsky, for the failure to report the dissemination of the litterateur Belinsky's letter that constitutes criminal offense against church and government and of the pernicious work of the lieutenant Grigoriev —to be deprived, on the basis of the Code of Military Decrees, Pt. V, Bk. 1, art. 142, 144, 169, 170, 172, 174, 176, 177 and 178, of ranks, of all rights concomitant to his social estate and to be subjected to the death penalty by shooting.

Decision of the High Military Court

The actions of each of the defendants consist of the following: [...]

13. Regarding the retired engineer-lieutenant Fyodor Dostoevsky (27 years old).

The lieutenant Dostoevsky, by his own admission, attending the meetings at Petrashevsky's for three years, heard the criminal opinions expressed there about, among other things, the emancipation of the peasants, about administrative changes in the judicial system, and himself took part in discussion about the severity of the censorship; at one meeting, in March of the current year, 1849, he read the letter of the litterateur Belinsky to Gogol which he had received from Moscow, from the defendant Pleshcheev, which was filled with impertinent remarks against the Orthodox Church and the Supreme Ruler. Then, seeing the approval this letter met with, Dostoevsky read it at the meetings at Durov's and then gave it to the defendant Mombelli to be copied. At those same meetings at Durov's he heard other liberal articles being read, knew about a proposal to establish a private lithography for the dissemination of articles directed against the government and, finally, he was at a luncheon at the home of the defendant Speshnev when the defendant Grigoriev read his subversive work entitled "Soldiers' Conversation."

During the investigation, Dostoevsky, admitting that he had indeed taken part in discussion about the possibility of some changes and improvements, answered that he expected them to come from the government; that he read Belinsky's letter at the meetings as a literary monument, being certain that he would not be leading anyone into temptation [...]

The charges against each of the defendants are based on their own testimony, on written documents found in their possession and on more or less positive evidence.

The degree of their guilt, based on the individual acts of criminal conspiracy detected, consists of the following: [...]

10. The retired engineer-lieutenant Dostoevsky (the litterateur) attended the meetings at Petrashevsky's and took part in the criminal discussion which took place there and in March of this year, having received from Moscow from the defendant Pleshcheev a copy of the criminal letter of the litterateur Belinsky, which is filled with impertinent remarks against the

Supreme Ruler and the Orthodox Church, read the letter at meetings at Durov's and Petrashevsky's, and then gave it to the defendant Mombelli to be copied; at the meetings at Durov's he took part in consultations aimed at writing articles opposing the government and disseminating them by means of a private lithography; finally, he was at a luncheon in the home of the defendant Speshnev at which was read lieutenant Grigoriev's article of subversive content, entitled "Soldiers' Conversation" [...]

The High Military Court, having examined the substance of the guilt of each of the defendants, concludes that while the degree of their guilt varies, some having been more, and others, less, involved in conspiracy, since they all were tried in accordance with the Criminal Field Code for state crimes, according to the precise authority of our laws no distinction is made between the major culprits and the accomplices; the High Military Court therefore decides, on the basis of this Code: for all the defendants, namely the titular counsellor Butashevich-Petrashevsky, the unemployed nobleman Speshnev,[27] the lieutenants Mombelli and Grigoriev, the staff-captain Lvov 2nd, the student Filippov, the candidate Akhsharumov,[28] the student Khanykov, the collegiate assessor Durov, the retired lieutenant Dostoevsky, the collegiate councillor Debu 1st, the collegiate secretary Debu 2nd, the teacher Toll, the titular counsellor Yastrzhembsky, the unemployed nobleman Pleshcheev, the titular counsellors Kashkin and Golovinsky, the lieutenant Palm, the titular counsellor Timkovsky, the collegiate secretary Evropeus and the *meshchanin* Shaposhnikov,[29] to be subjected to death penalty by shooting [...]

The High Military Court, having determined the degree of punishment for the defendants on the basis of the military field laws, was, however, unable not to take into consideration the extenuating circumstances which suggest mitigation of the lot of the defendants in the case, specifically, the signs of repentance given by many of them, the voluntary admission during the investigation to acts which without their frankness would not have been known, the young age at which they came under the influence of ill-intentioned conspiracy and, finally, the fact that their criminal undertakings did not result in any harmful consequences, since they were deterred by the timely measurés taken by the state.

Therefore, laying the lot of the defendants at the monarchic mercy of Your Royal Highness, the High Military Court, on the basis of the rules given for its guidance, takes the liberty of most humbly petitioning Him to determine, in place of the death penalty, punishment according to guilt, in the following gradations [...]

7. The retired lieutenant Dostoevsky, for the same participation in criminal conspiracy, for the dissemination of the letter of the litterateur Belinsky, which was filled with impudent remarks made against the Orthodox Church and Supreme Ruler, and for the attempt, made along with others, to disseminate works opposing the government by means of a private lithography,[30] should be deprived of all rights concomitant to his social estate

and exiled to a hard-labor prison camp for eight years.

Nicholas I's instructions: "For four years and then made a private."

The Imperially-Approved Plan
for Carrying out the Verdict
Against the Convicted Conspirators

On the Semenovsky Parade Ground, across from the middle of the rampart, three stakes are to be erected on an elevation of one arshin. No pit is to be dug.

Around them are to be arranged, in batallions, the Life Guards of the Regiment of Chasseurs and the Moscow Regiment and a batallion of Life Guards from the Cavalry-Grenadiers.

On the 22nd of December [1849], at nine in the morning, the criminals are to be transported to this place in carriages. In front of and behind the convoy are to be found platoons from the St. Petersburg Division of Gendarmes. The convoy is to proceed at a trot out of the fortress, across the Neva, onto the Gagarin Pier, along the embankment to the Arsenal, along Liteiny Prospect and Vladimirsky Street to the Semenovsky Parade Ground. At every carriage, on each side, there is to be one mounted gendarme and in front of the procession a mounted Drill Aide-de-Camp.

The criminals are to be transported right up to the troops. Once they have gotten out of the carriages, a priest in funeral vestments, holding a cross and Holy Gospel, is to meet them and lead them, under escort, past the troops, stopping across from the center of the troups.[32]

Once they have stopped in front of the troops, the lieutenants and sergeants are to be called to the center, commanded to present arms and the drummers are to sound three drum rolls and the sentence is to be read, according to the statute.

After the reading, the command is to be given to slope arms and for the lieutenants and sergeants to take their places and, with the drums beating, the ceremony is to be continued. The uniforms are to be removed from the noblemen and swords are to be broken over the heads of those who have been designated to be sent into penal servitude. Then all of the criminals are to be dressed in long white shirts (from Lieutenant Palm, the uniform is not be be removed, swords are not to be broken over him, nor is he to be dressed in a long shirt).[33] The priest is to give his blessing and move away.

To the stakes are to be led the criminals: *Petrashevsky, Mombelli* and *Grigoriev,* with eyes bound. After these criminals have been tied to the stakes, each is approached at a distance of fifteen paced by fifteen privates, accompanied by their sergeants, with loaded rifles. The other criminals remain by the escorts.

After this, the Imperial Ratification is to be carried out.

When this has been carried out, the criminals are to be dressed in warm clothing, Petrashevsky is to be shackled and taken from the site of sentencing with a gendarme and courier. The rest of the criminals are to return to the fortress and be dispatched by special orders.

All of the general orders for the conveyance of the criminals out of the fortress and for the fulfillment of the execution ceremony and for their removal from the site of sentencing are placed under the personal jurisdiction of the St. Petersburg Commandant.

His Majesty requests that the subsequent fulfillment of the Imperial Ratification be placed under the personal jurisdiction of General Aide-de-Camp Sumarokov.

Dostoevsky's Description of his Arrest
as Entered in O. A. Milyukova's Album

On the twenty-second, or rather, the twenty-third of April (1849) I returned home between three and four in the morning from Grigoriev's, went to bed and immediately fell asleep. No more than an hour later through my sleep I noticed that some suspicious and strange people had come into my room. A sabre rattled, having gotten caught on something. What on earth was going on? I struggle to open my eyes and hear a soft, pleasant voice say: "Get up!"

I look around: there is a precinct or district superintendant of police, with gorgeous sideburns. But he was not the one speaking; the one speaking was a gentleman dressed in light blue with a lieutenant-colonel's epaulettes.

"What is the matter?", I asked, getting up from bed.

"By imperial order..."

I look around: indeed it was "by imperial order." In the doorway stood a soldier in light blue. He was the owner of the sabre that had rattled.....
"Aha! So that's what's going on!" I thought.

"Allow me..." I started to say...

"It doesn't matter! Get dressed... We'll wait," added the lieutenant colonel in a still more pleasant voice.

While I was getting dressed, they demanded all my books and started rummaging around; they did not find many but they rummaged through everything. My papers and letters they bound neatly with a string. The superintendant of police displayed a great deal of ingenuity in this matter: he climbed up so he could reach into the stove and then groped around in the old ashes with my long-stemmed pipe. At his invitation, the petty officer from the gendarmerie stood on a chair and climbed up over the stove, but he lost hold of the cornice and crashed down onto the chair making a loud noise and then both fell to the ground. At this point the ingenuous gentlemen became convinced that there was nothing on top of the stove.

On the table there was a fifteen-copeck piece which was old and bent. The superintendant of police attentively examined it and finally nodded to the lieutenant-colonel.

"Well, aren't you worried about its being counterfeit?" I asked.

"Hm... That, in fact, must be looked into..." mumbled the superintendant and he ended up including it in the evidence.

We left. We were accompanied by my frightened landlady and her servant, Ivan, who despite the fact that he was very frightened had a dull air of ceremoniousness about him, befitting the occasion and, for that matter, the ceremoniousness was not very festive. By the entryway a carriage stood waiting; we got in: the soldier, myself, the superintendant and the colonel, then we drove off along the Fontanka toward the Tsepny Bridge by the Summer Garden.

When we got there, there were a lot of people and a lot of bustling about. I saw many of my acquaintances. Everyone was still half-asleep and quiet. Some gentleman, a civilian but with a high rank was receiving us... an uninterrupted flow of gentlemen in light-blue arrived with their various victims.

"Here's St. George's Day for you, old lady!" somebody muttered into my ear.[34]

And, in fact, the twenty-third of April was St. George's Day.

We gradually surrounded the civilian who had the list in his hands. On the list by Mr. Antonelli's name had been written in pencil: "agent for the given case."

"So it's Antonelli!" we thought.

We were relegated to various corners pending a final decision about where to put whom. In the so-called white hall seventeen of us were gathered.

Leonty Vasilevich entered...[35]

But here I shall interrupt my story. It's too long to tell. But I affirm that Leonty Vasilevich was a most agreeable man...

F. Dostoevsky
May 24, 1860

A. N. Maikov's Letter to P. A. Viskovatov (1885)

I was in fact implicated in the Petrash[evsky] case, and I can legitimately say that to this day nobody has sound knowledge of this case; what the "case" and testimony revealed is all nonsense; what was of serious consequence did not reach the Commission. Indeed, I have told you about this. I became acquainted with Petrashevsky at the university and then would occasionally go to his house, first of all because all of us young fellows knew each other and also because it was fun. On account of the death of my brother (in the summer of 1847), which left me deeply shaken, and at the time being also swept up in the passionate beginnings of my romance with Anna Ivanovna, I went to Petrash(evsky's) only once more, in December of 1847. My brother had become diverted from Petrash(evsky's) circle way before, when he received the post as critic for *Notes of the Fatherland,* and his own circle had formed around him: Vlad(imir) Miliutin, Stasov, and three or four more people. Whereas I was occupied with my romance and specifically with what it necessitated—making as much money as possible, which meant that I sat at my desk writing Italian stories and then criticism for *Notes of the Fatherland,* and thus was off on my own, isolated from everyone. Once, it seems to me that it was in January of 1848,[36] F. M. Dostoevsky came to my house and spent the night—at the time I was living on my own in an apartment—my bed was against the wall, across from it was the couch where a bed was laid for Dostoevsky. And then he starts to tell me that he had been commissioned to make a proposal to me: Petrashevsky, he said, was a fool, and actor and a chatterbox; nothing sound would come out of him and so those among his guests who meant business had conceived of a project that was unknown to Petrashevsky and that would not include him, and namely: Speshnev, Pav(el) Filippov (since these two are dead, I refer to them by name, I think that the others are still alive and for this reason I will pass over them in silence just as I have been silent about this episode for thirty-seven years) and five or maybe six others, I do not recall the exact number, among them Dostoevsky. They had decided to try to enlist a seventh or eighth, namely, me. They had decided to establish a secret typography, publish and so forth. I tried to point out how emptyheaded and disturbing such an affair was and that they were headed for certain disaster. And besides—and this was my major argument— you (F.M.)

and I are poets and hence impractical folk, we cannot even manage our own affairs whereas political activity constitutes the highest degree of practicality, etc. And I remember how D(ostoevsky), sitting there like the dying Socrates before his friends, in a nightshirt with the neck unbuttoned, waxed eloquent on the sacred nature of the project, on our duty to save the fatherland and so forth—so that I finally started laughing and joking. "So that means no?" he concluded. "No, a thousand times no." The next morning after tea, he said as he was leaving: "I do not need to tell you not to breathe a word about this to anyone." "That goes without saying." Subsequently I learned that a manual printing press had been ordered piece by piece from sketches made up by Filippov and commissioned in different parts of the city and that a day or two before the arrests it was brought and assembled in the apartment of one of the participants, M(ordvino)v, whom I do not think I knew: when he was arrested and his house searched, no attention was paid to the press since he had all sorts of scientific and other types of instruments and apparatus in his study, however, the door was sealed. When the Commission departed and M(ordvinov) was escorted away, his family managed, without damaging the seals, to take the door off the hinges and they got rid of the press. In this manner, the evidence was destroyed. The Commission did not know about this project, nor did Petrashevsky, and of those who escaped arrest I was the only one to know. So, if I was tormented as I awaited arrest (which I expected because of my close relations with Dost[oevsky] and Pleshcheev) and if later I was even more afraid once at my interrogation at the fortress, then it was precisely because of this secret visit paid me by Dost(oevsky) and of what he had imparted to me. But at my interrogation I was not asked about it and I quite freely and casually responded all about Fourier's theory, the phan-lansteries, doing so not without a bit of humor, the members laughing when I sketched out the type of barrack-like quarters they would be, where my cell would be and how all life would be out in the open for all eyes to see and how no amorous intrigue could remain secret. I expatiated upon Dost(oevsky)'s difficult nature, describing how he had broken with everybody except me and how of late he had even cooled toward me so that we saw each other less. I maintained my acquaintance with Petrash(evsky) out of courtesy and because it was amusing. When I was at last told: "you may go—you are free," I at last breathed a sigh of relief and I began to feel terribly cheerful in particular about the fact that I had been asked nothing about "that night." I remember that when I went out of the well-lit room where the Commission sat and into the dark corridor where I suddenly found myself alone in the darkness, I started off in a random direction; it occurred to me to go back to the general's and ask that I be shown the way out, when suddenly I stumbled upon somebody walking along and with my hand which I held out in front of me I felt something metallic like a star and suddenly I heard a stern voice: "Who is that? Where are you going?" A candle appeared from somewhere and I saw that I had walked past the guard and that in front of me was a general in full dress uniform—it was, as I learned later, Commander Nabokov: "I am on my way from the Commission, I was told that I am free,—so I set off but I do not know which way to go." He pointed out the way and I found myself in the courtyard of the fortress, clearly lit by the moon—and there was not a soul there! Again I did not know which way to go." He pointed out the way and I found myself in the courtyard of the fortress, which was clearly lit by the moon—and there was not a soul there! Again, I did not know which way to head. I stood and looked at the cathedral. Everything was quiet and there within the walls were my acquaintances but what was happening to them? I still did not have any idea of what they had gotten themselves in for. Thank God I had not been asked about the typography: what would I have said? It must be said that in my responses there was no falsehood of any sort and nothing to cast an accusing shadow on anybody. Immediately Dubelt set me completely at my ease and made me feel almost casual; his first smile had let loose my sense of humor—of Petrashevsky, for example, I said that he always gave us a laugh: once he had arrived at our summer house during a thunderstorm in the middle of the night—we had already gotten undressed—and there he was in a Spanish raincoat and bandit hat. Of Dost(toevsky) I said with emotion and regret that I had quarrelled with him and that he habitually quarrelled with people because of his great conceit and his difficult nature. Finally, while I was still in the fortress, I bumped into the same gendarme officer, from a modest background, who had escorted me from the Third Department to the fortress and who until my summons to the Commission had guarded me in the warden's room and when I was in there looking at the scenes of Venice that were hanging on the walls, I started to tell him how there you had an odd city, with no horses, no streets, only canals and how cooks would have to get their provisions either by going by boat or by waiting for the merchants to come up in boats and they would lower baskets with money and the merchants would load them with provisions—and he looked at me as if I were a liar and maybe even a dangerous one. "So, you got me in here, now show me how to get out," I said to him. He shared my joy as if he were a close relative or friend and said: "Let's go! Let's go!" He had a driver waiting for him. "What is this," I said, "when you brought me here you thought I was God knows what kind of criminal and now here you yourself are glad." "Such is the nature of the job—when you bring someone in, you do not know, you are afraid, but now it is another matter. Why don't you come home with me for some tea and a bite to eat, it's late." "No, I thank you most humbly, we'll reach the carriage and then you must drop me off so I can set my parents at rest." Naturally, I went to see my parents and at daybreak sent a note to Anna Ivanovna.

However, in sitting down to write you this letter, I had no idea that I would end up telling you this story. For I still feel somewhat bound by my word given "that night" to Dost(oevsky). Yet, at some point I will describe it all in more order and detail.

A.N. Maikov's Account of his Implication in the Petrashevsky Affair, As Recorded by A. A. Golenishchev-Kutuzov

I was at Maikov's (Ap(ollon) Nik(olaevich)'s) and he told me the story of his participation in the Petrashevsky affair (1849).

Here is his story:

I am lying in bed one morning. A gendarme officer appears along with a civilian. He asks : "Are you A. N. Maikov?"

"I am."

"Kindly get dressed. We will first perform a search and then ask that you accompany us. Avez-vous des livres défendus?"

"Probablement."

"Où sont-ils?"

"Mais voilà toute ma bibliothèque, cherchez" and so forth.

Tea was drunk; my notebooks and papers were gone through and we set off by carriage for the Third Department. There they assigned me a room, treated me very politely , and served luncheon. Then I quite calmly went to sleep. At ten in the evening I was awakened and conducted to the fortress under guard. I was escorted by some officer, who had obviously worked his way up through the ranks, and he did not say a word the whole time. I was taken to the fortress and led through the dark corridors until I was finally led into a spacious, well-lit room with a table, covered in red or green cloth (I do not remember), behind which sat some generals. Dubelt very courteously told me to take a seat and he put forth the points of interrogation:

"Were you acquainted with Petrashevsky?"

"I was. We graduated from the university together and I knew him just as I knew all our other fellow-students."

"So write—as briefly as possible something like *university acquaintance*. Did the acquaintance continue afterwards?"

"At first it did not since I had left Petersburg and was abroad, but then upon my return we met and he invited me to his Friday gatherings. I had no reason to keep from going. A diverse group would gather at Petrashevsky's; it was fairly pleasant and even sometimes amusing since Petrashevsky *vive forceur* imparted to his Fridays the appearance of some kind of conference."

"And even presided with a bell?"

"Yes. My brother and I would go there and often laughed at them but we continued to go out of curiosity and so as not to offend an old crony."

"So write that briefly. *We continued the acquaintance for the sake of politeness.* Do you know Fourier's doctrine, do you approve of it?"

"Of course I know it, but mainly second hand. But do I approve of it? Of course not. The phalansteries appear to me to be somehow extremely dull, ugly and inconvenient. First of all, it would be a pity to destroy our towns only to live in barracks, along a corridor, in a cell—no, I humbly thank you; if you do not have a home of your own you might as well be living on the street! For a young man it is extremely annoying for everybody to know who comes calling on him!"

Laughter breaks out all around and I appear to have won everyone over.

But then they posed what was for me the most difficult, grave and delicate question.

"Were you acquainted with Dostoevsky (Fyodor Mikhailovich) and what were your relations with him?"

The question was grave because I had no idea of the extent to which he had been implicated and of what he had testified, whereas Dostoevsky and I had had a very important conversation.

One evening Dostoevsky comes to see me in my apartment in the Anichkov building, he is all excited and says that he has an important message for me.

"You of course understand," he said, "that Petrashevsky is a chatterbox, a lightweight and that nothing sound will come out of his escapades. And so some more serious people from his circle decided to go off on their own (but secretly and without letting the others know) and form their own special secret society with a secret typography for the printing of various books and even journals if possible. We had our doubts about you because you are too conceited." (Here was Fyodor Mikhailovich, of all people, accusing me of conceit!)

"How so?"

"You refuse to accept authority, for example, you did not agree with Speshnev" (who had preached Fourierism).

"Political economy does not particularly interest me. But, still, it seems to me that what Speshnev says is nonsense; but so what?"

"For a common cause one has to be able to restrain oneself. There are seven of us: Speshnev, Mordvinov, Mombelli, Pavel Filippov, Grigorev, Vladimir Milyutin and myself—we decided on you as the eighth; do you want to join the group?

"But to what end?"

"Naturally, with the purpose of bringing about an upheaval in Russia. We already have a printing press; it was ordered in parts from various places, according to Mordvinov's sketches; everything is ready."

"I not only have no desire to join your group but I also advise you to renounce it. What kind of political activists are we? We are poets, artists, not practical people and we are without a penny to our names. Are we cut out to be revolutionaries?"

Dostoevsky started to preach passionately and lengthily, gesticulating in his red nightshirt with the neck undone.

We argued for a long time and finally got tired and went to bed.

In the morning Dostoevsky asked: "Well, what about it?"

"The same as yesterday. I woke up before you and was thinking. I myself will not join, and I repeat —if there still is a chance— dump them and leave their midst."

"Well, that is my business. But keep one thing in mind: only seven other people know about everything that was said yesterday. You are the ninth— there must not be a tenth!"

"As for that, here, we will shake on it! I will keep still about it."

This was the conversation we had had and this was why it was difficult for me to answer.

I said that I knew Dostoevsky and liked him very much, that he was a good man and nice fellow, but unbelievely conceited and difficult, that he had quarrelled with everyone after the success of his "Poor Folk" and that only with me had there not been any quarrels to speak of but that in the past years (I deliberately exaggerated the time a bit, yet after that conversation we had in fact hardly seen each other) Dostoevsky had cooled toward me and we hardly saw each other.

After that some insignificant questions were put to me and I was informed that I was free and could go home. I went out into the dark corridor and having lost my way, I bumped into someone who suddenly asked in a threatening tone: "Who's there?" A door opened and General Nabokov appeared (a nice but gruff old man).

"What are you doing here?"

I explained and I was escorted to the street. There I met the gendarme officer who had brought me there and who, upon finding out that I had been set free turned out to be very talkative and kindhearted person, who sincerely rejoiced at my being set free. I returned to my apartment and my papers and books were soon returned to me.

Whether the Investigatory Commission knew about this faction of the Petrashevsky group—I do not know. When Dostoevsky's verdict was pronounced, among the charges against him was "the intention of opening a secret typography." During the search at Mordvinov's, where the press was kept, it did not attract any attention because it was in his laboratory along with assorted equipment, retorts, and so forth. The room was sealed off and his relatives managed, without breaking the seal, to take the door off its hinges and removed the ill-starred press.

Epilogue. In 1855, after Alexander II ascended to the throne, one fine day some strange and rather unseemly individual appears on the scene and starts to congratulate me.

"Who are you and why the congratulations?"

"I am an agent of the secret police and I am congratulating you for having been removed from police surveillance."

"You mean I was under surveillance?"

"Of course; we have been making notes about you all the time."

"And what have you been writing?"

"Everything, from day to day we've known everything."

"And were you satisfied with me?"

"For pity's sake! Couldn't have been more pleased."

I gave him a ruble; he disappeared and thus the whole business of my implication in the Petrashevsky conspiracy came to a close.

Dostoevsky's Letters to his Brother Mikhail

18 July 1849. Petersburg. Peter-Paul Fortress

I was gladdened beyond words, dear brother, by your letter. I received it July 11. You're finally free,[1] and I can imagine what happiness it was for you to see your family. How they must have been waiting for you! I see that you're beginning to get yourself fixed up along new lines. What are you doing now, and most important, what are you living on? Do you have work, and what precisely are you doing? Summer in the city is depressing! And in addition, you say that you've taken another apartment and you're probably more crowded. It's a pity that you can't finish the rest of the summer out of town.

Thank you for the packages; they've given me great relief and amusement. You write, dear brother, that I should not be despondent. But I'm not despondent; of course, I'm bored and miserable, but what can be done? But I'm not even always bored. All in all, my time goes along extremely unevenly—sometimes too quickly, and then it drags. At other times you even feel that you seem to have gotten used to such a life and that it doesn't make any difference. I of course chase temptations from my imagination, but sometimes you can't cope with them, and one's former life simply forces its way into the soul, and the past is relived again. But that's in the nature of things. The days are clear now, at least for the most part, and it's grown a bit more cheerful. But inclement days are unbearable, the casemate looks more grim. I have some pursuits, too. I haven't lost any time, I've thought up three stories and two novels; one of them I'm writing now,[2] but I'm afraid to work a lot.

This work, especially if it is done with enthusiasm (and I have never worked so con amore as now), always exhausted me, irritating my nerves. When I worked at freedom, I constantly needed to interrupt myself with diversions, but here the agitation after writing has to pass on its own. My health is good, except for my hemorrhoids and the derangement of my nerves, which is proceeding at a crescendo. I've begun having throat spasms, as before, my appetite is very slight, and I get little sleep, and even at that with painful dreams. I sleep about five hours in twenty-four and wake up about four times a night. That's the only thing that's depressing. The hardest thing is the time when night falls, and at 9 o'clock it's already dark here. I sometimes can't get to sleep until one or two a.m., so that enduring five hours or so of darkness is depressing. That undoes my health more than anything else.

I can't tell you anything about the time of the conclusion of our case, because I've already lost all reckoning, and I just keep a calendar in which I passively note each passing day—phew! I've read a little bit here: two journeys to holy places and the works of St. Dmitri of Rostov. The last interested me very much; but that reading is a drop in the ocean, and I think I would be unbelievably happy to receive a book. The more so as it will even be curative, because you refashion your own thoughts using other people's or rethink your own along new lines.

That's all the details about my life; there's nothing else. I'm very glad that you found your family well. Have you written to Moscow about your release? It's a great pity that the business there is not being resolved. How I would love to spend even a single day with you! It will soon be three months that we have been incarcerated; what will happen after this? Perhaps you won't even see the green leaves this summer. Do you remember how they sometimes took us out to walk in the little garden in May? The greenery was just beginning then, and I was reminded of Revel, where I used to visit you at about that time, and the garden in the Engineering Building. I kept thinking that you would make that comparison too—it was so sad. I'd like to see a few other people too. Whom are you seeing now; everyone must be out in the country. Our brother Andrei certainly must be in town; have you seen Nikolya.[3] Give my regards to them. Kiss all the children for me, give my regards to your wife, tell her that I'm very touched that she remembers me, and don't worry about me much. I only desire to be healthy, and boredom is a passing matter, and besides, good spirits depend on me alone. There is a huge amount of malleability and vitality in man, and I really didn't think that there was so much, but now I've learned from experience. Well, good-bye! Here are a couple of words from me, and I hope that they give you pleasure. Give my regards to everyone you see and whom I knew, don't neglect anyone. I have been recollecting everyone. What do the children think about me and I'm curious what assumptions they're making about me: where, for instance, has he disappeared to! Well, good-bye. If you can, send me *Notes of the Fatherland*. You'll read anything. Write a couple of words, too. That will make me extraordinarily happy.

Good-bye.

18 July

Your brother F. Dostoevsky.

Notes

1. Mikhail had been released from the Peter-Paul Fortress June 24, 1849.
2. "The Little Hero."
3. Nikolai Mikhailovich Dostoevsky.

14 September 1849. Petersburg. Peter-Paul Fortress

I received your letter, dear brother, the books (Shakespeare, the Bible, *Notes of the Fatherland*), and the money (10 silver rubles), and I thank you for all of that. I'm glad that you're well. I'm still the same as before. The same upset stomach and hemorrhoids. I really don't know when this will pass. The difficult autumn months are approaching, and with them my acute depression. Now the sky is already glowering, but the bright bit of sky visible from my casemate is a guarantee of my health and good spirits. But still and all, for the meanwhile I'm still alive and well. And for me that's quite a fact. And therefore please don't think anything especially bad about me. For the time being everything is fine in regard to my health. I expected much worse and now I see that there is so much vitality stored up in me that you can't exhaust it.

I thank you again for the books. They're at least a diversion. It's been nearly five months now that I've been living on my own means, that is, on my head along and nothing else. For the time being the machine has not yet come unstrung and is still functioning. Constant thinking, however, and just thinking, without any outside impressions to revive and support thought is hard going! It's as though I were under an air pump from which the air is being pumped out. Everything in me has gone to my head, and from my head to thought, everything, absolutely everything, and in spite of that this work increases with every day. Books, even though only a drop in the ocean, still help. But work itself seems only to drain my last juices from me. I'm glad for it, however.

I've read through the books that you sent. I thank you especially for Shakespeare. How did you guess! The English novel[1] in *Notes of the Fatherland* is extraordinarily good. But Turgenev's comedy[2] is unpardonably bad. How did this misfortune come about? Can it really be that he is definitely fated after all to spoil every one of his works that exceeds a signature sheet in size? I didn't recognize him in that comedy. No originality: an old, beaten track. All of this has been said before him and much better than by him. The last scene reeks of infantile weakness. There are flashes of something here and there, but that something is good only by virtue of the lack of anything better. What an excellent piece about banks! And how accessible to everyone!

I thank everyone who remembers about me. Give my regards to Emilia Fyodorovna,[3] our brother Andrei, and kiss the children, whom I especially wish good health. I really don't know, brother, how and when we'll see each other. Good-bye and please don't forget me. Write me in at least two weeks.

Good-bye.

Your F. Dostoevsky

14 Sept. 49

Please don't be so worried about me. If you find anything to read, send it.

Notes

1. Emily Bronte's *Jane Eyre.*

2. *The Bachelor* (1849). It is worth noting that Turgenev's comedy shows the influence of Dostoevsky's *Poor Folk,* especially in the two central protagonists.

3. Mikhail Dostoevsky's wife.

22 December 1849. Petersburg. Peter-Paul Fortress

Peter-Paul Fortress
22 December

Brother, my dear brother! Everything has been decided! I have been sentenced to four years of labor in a fortress (Orenburg, I think) and then to the ranks.[1] Today, December 22, we were taken to Semyonov Square. There we were all read the death sentence, allowed to kiss the cross, had sabers broken over our heads and our pre-death attire put on (white shirts). Then three people were stood against the stakes for the carrying out of the execution. I was the sixth in line, people were summoned by threes, cons[equently], I was in the second row and had no more than a minute left to live. I remembered you, brother, and all of your family; at the last moment you, only you, were in my mind, only then did I realize how much I love you, my dear brother! I had time also to embrace Pleshcheev, Durov, who were nearby, and to say farewell to them. Finally a retreat was sounded, the ones tied to the stake were led back, and it was announced that His Imperial Majesty was granting us our lives. Then the real sentences followed. *Palm* alone was pardoned. He'll go back into the army with the same rank.

I've just been told, dear brother, that we're to set off today or tomorrow. I asked to see you. But I was told that was impossible;[2] I can only write you this letter, which you should hurry to give me a response to. I'm afraid that you might somehow have known of our sentences (to death). From the windows of the wagon, when we were being taken to Semyonov Square, I saw a throng of people; perhaps the news had already reached you too and you were suffering for me. Now you'll be able to feel better for me. Brother! I'm not despondent and I haven't lost heart. Life is everywhere, life is in ourselves, and not outside. There will be people by my side, and to be a *human being* among people and to remain one forever, no matter in what circumstances, not to grow despondent and not to lose heart—that's what life is all about, that's its task. I have come to recognize that. That idea has entered my flesh and blood. But it's the truth! The head that created, lived the higher life of art, that recognized and grew accustomed to the higher demands of the spirit, that head has already been cut from my shoulders. What remains is memory and images created and not yet embodied by me. They will ulcerate me, really! But there remain in me a heart and the same flesh and blood that can also love, and suffer, and pity, and remember, and that's life, too! On voit le soleil [One can see the sun]![3]

Well, good-bye, brother! Don't grieve about me! Now about the disposition of things: the books (the Bible has remained with me) and several sheets of my manuscript (the rough plan for a drama and a novel and the finished story "A Child's Fairy Tale"[4]) have been taken from me and in all likelihood will wind up with you. I'm also leaving my coat and old clothes, if you'll come to pick them up. Now, brother, I'm faced with what may be a long journey to prison. I need money. Dear brother, as soon as you receive this letter, and if you can get money, send it to me immediately. I need money now more than I do air (because of a special circumstance). Send me a few lines from you too. Then, if the Moscow money[5] comes through, look after my interests and don't abandon me... Well, that's all. There are debts, but what can be done about them?!

Kiss your wife and children. Remind them about me; see to it that they don't forget me. Perhaps we'll see each other sometime? Brother, take care of yourself and your family, live quietly and with foresight. Think about your children's future... Live positively.

Never before have such abundant and healthy reserves of spiritual life teemed in me as now. But I don't know whether my body will endure it. I'm setting out unwell, I have scrofula. But perhaps somehow! Brother! I have already experienced so much in life that there's very little that will frighten me. Let come what may! I'll let you hear from me at the first possible opportunity.

Give the Maikovs farewell and final greetings from me. Tell them that I thank them all for their constant concern for my fate. Say a few words for me, as warm as possible, whatever your heart dictates, to Yevgeniya Petrovna.[6] I wish her much happiness and will always remember her with grateful respect. Shake Nikolai Apollonovich's and Apollon Maikov's hands for me, and then everyone's.

Find Yanovsky.[7] Shake his hand and thank him. Finally, shake the hand of everyone who hasn't forgotten me. And remind those who have. Kiss our brother *Kolya.* Write a letter to our brother Andrei and tell him about me. Write our uncle and aunt.[8] Write to our sisters: I wish them happiness!

But perhaps we'll even see each other, brother. Take care of yourself, live, for Heaven's sake, until we can meet each other. Perhaps we'll embrace each other some time and recall our young, our past golden time, our youth and our hopes, which at this moment I am tearing out of my heart with blood and am burying.

Can it be that I'll never take pen in hand? I think that in 4 years it will be possible. I'll send you everything I write if I write anything. My God! How many images, cast out, created by me anew will perish, will expire in my head or contaminate my blood like a poison! Yes, if I won't be able to write, I'll perish. Better fifteen years of imprisonment and a pen in hand!

Write me often, in great detail, a lot, and fully. Go on at length in every letter about your family details, about trivialities, don't forget that. That will give me hope and life. If you only knew how your letters enlivened me here in the casemate. These two-and-a-half months (last), when correspondence was forbidden, were very difficult for me. I was unwell. The fact that you didn't send any money from time to time worried me to death about you: evidently you were in great need yourself! Kiss the children one more time; their dear little faces don't leave my head. Oh, may they be happy! May you be happy, too, brother, be happy!

But don't grieve, for Heaven's sake, don't grieve about me! Know that I haven't lost heart, remember that hope has not abandoned me. In four years there will be an easing of my lot. I'll be a common soldier—no longer a prisoner, and keep in mind that someday I'll embrace you. After all I was at death's door today, I lived with that thought for three-quarters of an hour, I faced the last moment, and now I'm alive again![9]

If anyone remembers me with malice, and if I quarrelled with anyone, if I made a bad impression on anyone—tell them to forget about that if you manage to see them. There is no bile or spite in my soul, I would like to love and embrace at least someone out of the past at this moment. It's a comfort, I experienced it today while saying farewell to my dear ones before death. At that moment I thought that the news of the execution would kill you. But now be calm, I'm still alive and will live in the future with the thought that someday I'll embrace you. That's the only thing I have in my thoughts now.

What are you doing? What did you think today? Do you know about us? How cold it was today!

Oh, if only my letter would reach you soon. Otherwise I'll be without news of you for about four months. I saw the packages in which you sent money the last two months; the address was written in your hand, and I was glad that you were well.

When I look back at the past and think about how much time was spent in vain, how much of it was lost in delusions, in errors, in idleness, in the inability to live; how I failed to value it, how many times I sinned against my heart and spirit—then my heart contracts in pain. Life is a gift, life is happiness, each moment could have been an eternity of happiness. Si jeunesse savait! [If youth knew!] Now, changing my life, I'm being regenerated into a new form. Brother! I swear to you that I won't lose hope and will preserve my heart and spirit in purity. I'll be reborn for the better. That's my entire hope, my entire consolation.

Life in the casemate has already sufficiently killed off in me the needs of the flesh that were not completely pure; before that I took little care of myself. Now deprivations no longer bother me in the slightest, and therefore don't be afraid that material hardship will kill me. That can't be. Oh, if only my health holds out!

Good-bye, good-bye, brother! When will I write to you again! You'll receive from me as detailed a report as possible about my journey. If only I can preserve my health, everything else will be all right!

Well, good-bye, good-bye, brother! I embrace you firmly, kiss you soundly. Remember me without pain in your heart. Don't be sad, please don't be sad about me! In my very next letter I'll write you about how things are. Remember what I've told you: calculate your life, don't waste it, put your fate in order, think about the children.—Oh, to see you someday! Good-bye! Now I'm tearing myself away from everything that was dear to me; it's painful to leave it! It's painful to break yourself in two, to tear your heart in half. Good-bye! Good-bye! But I'll see you, I'm certain, I hope, don't change, love me, don't let your memory grow cold, and the thought of your love will be the best part of life for me. Good-bye, once more good-bye! Good-bye to everyone!

Your brother Fyodor Dostoevsky

22 December 49

At the time of my arrest several books were taken away from me. Of them only two were forbidden. Won't you get the rest of them for yourself? But here's a request: of those books one was *The Works of Valerian Maikov,* his criticism—Yevgenia Petrovna's copy. She had given it to me as her priceless treasure. During my arrest I asked an officer of the gendarmes to give the book back to her and gave him the address. I don't know whether he returned it to her. Check on that! I don't want to take that memory away from her. Good-bye, once again good-bye.

Your F. Dostoevsky

I don't know whether I'll be walking or riding to prison. Riding I think. I hope!

Once more: shake Emilia Fyodorovna's hand and kiss the children.— Give my regards to Kraevsky, perhaps...

Write me in detail about your arrest, imprisonment, and release.

Notes

1. Dostoevsky served his term of labor at the Omsk Fortress, not Orenburg.

2. Dostoevsky was allowed to see his brother Mikhail on December 24, the day of his departure for Siberia.

3. A partially distorted quotation from Victor Hugo's "Le Dernier Jour d'un condamné" ["The Last Day of a Condemned Man"], a work several echoes of which may be found in the present letter.

4. A reference to the story "A Little Hero."

5. A reference to money from the sale of the Dostoevsky family estate.

6. Yevgenia Petrovna Maikova.

7. Stepan Dmitrievich Yanovsky (1815-1897), a doctor and close friend of Dostoevsky's. Their relations became somewhat strained in the 1860s, but the two continued to see each other.

8. The Kumanins.

9. Dostoevky used his recollections of those three-quarters of an hour at death's door in Prince Myshkin's protest against the death penalty in *The Idiot*.

Translations of Dostoevsky's letters to his brother Mikhail by David A. Lowe. Excerpted from Fyodor Dostoevsky, *Complete Letters,* volume 1 (Ann Arbor: Ardis, forthcoming).

Appendices

The explanatory material has been divided into three sections. The first identifies the people involved in the case (defendants, witnesses, associates of Dostoevsky's, prosecutors, etc.) who are mentioned in Dostoevsky's testimony and the related documents. The second section describes the ideologies, books and documents, mentioned in Dostoevsky's testimony, the alleged dissemination of which constituted, from the point of view of the prosecution, the *corpus delicti* in the case. The third section consists of notes clarifying specific passages in the text.

The identifications and notes are based on the notes in volume 18 of Dostoevsky's *Complete Works* (Leningrad: Nauka, 1978) and on the notes in N. F. Belchikov's *Dostoevskii v protsesse petrashevtsev* (Moscow: Nauka, 1971).

I: Identification of Persons Involved in the Case

Akhsharumov, Dmitry Dmitrievich (1823-1910): employed in the Asiatic Department of the Ministry of Foreign Affairs. Among those arrested for their participation in the Petrashevsky circle, he was the first to offer testimony to imply that the circle desired political and social upheaval. Although he later regretted his testimony, he explained that at the time he felt that their guilt was being exaggerated and therefore decided to be frank, thinking to himself: "If they actually knew the whole truth, then, perhaps, they would calm down." His death sentence was commuted to service in the penal battalions.

Antonelli, Petr Dmitrievich (1825-?): a student at Petersburg University whom I. P. Liprandi, an assistant to the Minister of Internal Affairs, recruited in 1848 to infiltrate the Petrashevsky circle. Petrashevsky never fully trusted Antonelli. Dostoevsky, in the description of his arrest, notes that the authorities let it be known to the defendants from the outset that Antonelli had been the informer. It has been suggested that L. V. Dubelt, the Director of the Third Department and Chief of Staff of the Corps of Gendarmes, who took over the case from the Ministry of Internal Affairs, days before the arrests, allowed this information to be revealed to the defendants in an attempt to discredit the preliminary work in the investigation done by Liprandi. Antonelli was soon forced to leave Petersburg because of widespread knowledge, and resentment, of his role in the affair.

Balasoglo, Alexander Panteliemonovich (1813-?): employed in the archive of the Asiatic Department of the Ministry of Foreign Affairs. He was known as an active member of the Petrashevsky circle and is recorded to have expressed particularly enthusiastic approval of Belinsky's letter to Gogol, which he heard Dostoevsky read. He was not tried.

Beletsky, Petr Ivanovich (1819-?): a history teacher at the 2nd Military School. He attended the meetings at Petrashevsky's but was not tried. He was, however, exiled to Vologda for insulting Antonelli, the informant, when he met him on the street.

Berestov, Alexei Ivanovich (1814-?): an artist, employed by the Commission for the Publication of Descriptions of the Uniforms and Armaments of the Russian Military Forces. He was not tried and had no connection with Dostoevsky.

Chernosvitov, Rafail Alexandrovich (1810-?): a retired officer, employed in government service in Siberia. He attended Petrashevsky's gatherings when he was in the capital. He was so outspoken in his speeches opposing the government that he caused Petrashevsky, Dostoevsky and others to suspect that he was an agent of the Third Department. According to Antonelli, Petrashevsky hoped to use Chernosvitov to bring about rebellion in Siberia.

Chirikov, Mikhail Nikolaevich (1803-?): a civil servant employed at the State Commercial Bank. He lodged at Petrashevsky's but was not tried.

Danilevsky, Nikolai Yakovlevich (1822-85): a botanist who attended Petrashevsky's circle where he was known to be the best-versed in Fourier's doctrine. During the winter of 1848, he took part in a conversation with Dostoevsky, Speshnev and Pleshcheev about the possibility of publishing banned books abroad. He was arrested; he did not stand trial, although he was sent away from the capital.

In the 1860s he became an important ideologue in the Slavophile movement, his main work in the field being entitled "Russia and Europe." Danilevsky commanded the respect of Dostoevsky, who was impressed with the manner in which this former Fourierist later demonstrated his love for Russia.

Debu (Desbut) 1, Konstantin Matveevich (1810-?): a translator in the Asiatic Department of the Ministry of Foreign Affairs. Along with his younger brother, he participated in the Petrashevsky circle. His death sentence was commuted to four years in a penal battalion.

Debu (Desbut) 2, Ippolit Matveevich (1824-90): a civil servant in the Asiatic Department of the Ministry of Foreign Affairs. His death sentence, received for his participation in the Petrashevsky circle, was, like his brother's, commuted to service in a penal battalion. Late in his life, he provided Dostoevsky's biographer, O. F. Miller, with information about Dostoevsky's participation in the Petrashevsky affair.

Deev, Platon Alexandrovich (1824-?): a student at Petersburg University. He lodged at Petrashevsky's but was not brought to trial.

Dostoevsky, Mikhail Mikhailovich (1820-64): Dostoevsky's older brother. A close bond existed between the two brothers who collaborated, during the period after Fyodor's return from exile and before Mikhail's death, as editors of the journals *Epokha* (The Epoch) and *Vremia* (Time). Mikhail Dostoevsky participated in the Petrashevsky circle and the smaller Durov circle but took a less active role than his brother. (He was not involved in the plot to establish the clandestine printing press.) He was arrested in conjunction with the case, somewhat later than most due to the fact that Andrei, a younger Dostoevsky brother, was mistakenly arrested in his place. Mikhail Dostoevsky was released two months later. Fyodor Dostoevsky, who felt responsible for his brother's involvement with the Petrashevsky group, took every opportunity in his testimony to indicate his brother's innocence and passive role in the circles. Writing years later (in *Diary of a Writer*) Fyodor Dostoevsky described his brother as having been an enthusiastic Fourierist in 1849.

Dubelt, Leonty Vasilevich (1792-1862): the director of the Third Department and Chief of Staff of the Corps of Gendarmes. On April 20, 1849, Dubelt took over the Petrashevsky case from Liprandi, an assistant to the Minister of Internal affairs, who with the help of Antonelli had been collecting information. Dubelt appears to have resented not having been involved in the case sooner. During the investigation, Dubelt impressed many of those being interrogated (among them, Dostoevsky and Maikov) as being a pleasant man.

Durov, Sergei Fyodorovich (1816-69): a poet, prose-writer and translator. He and Palm hosted the gatherings of a circle which broke off from the Petrashevsky group; it included Mombelli, Pleshcheev, Filippov, Speshnev and the two Dostoevskys, among others. In their testimony, its members insisted on its literary and musical orientation. Durov received a death sentence which was commuted to penal servitude. He and Dostoevsky were taken to Siberia in the same convoy and served together for a period, although their relations deteriorated.

Filippov, Pavel Nikolaevich (1825-55): a former student at Petersburg University. Filippov participated in the Petrashevsky circle and was introduced by Dostoevsky into the Durov circle. When attention of the Investigatory Commission was focused on Filippov's proposal to lithograph articles of a liberal nature, Dostoevsky did his best to defuse this proposal by attributing it to Filippov's impulsive personality rather than to political conviction. Filippov participated in the plot to establish a private printing press. He was sentenced to death, but his sentence was commuted to service in the penal battalions. Upon his departure from the Peter-Paul Fortress where the defendants were held prior to being sent to their various destinations, Filippov left twenty-five rubles with the officer in charge to be given to Dostoevsky, who was very much touched by this gesture. Filippov died of wounds received during his service.

Golovinsky, Vasily Andreevich (1829-?): a civil servant with legal background. Golovinsky was known in the Petrashevsky circle as an ardent advocate of the peasant cause. The Investigatory Commission focused attention on a speech made by him at Petrashevsky's on April 1, 1849, in which he discussed the emancipation of the serfs, freedom of the press and judicial reform. Remarks he made about the likelihood of an insurrection particularly disturbed the Investigatory Commission. Dostoevsky had borrowed a banned book, Proudhon's *Célébration du dimanche*, from Golovinsky. Golovinsky received a death sentence which was commuted to military service. (Golovinsky remained actively committed to aiding the serfs in the period prior to their emancipation in 1861.)

Grigoriev, Nikolai Petrovich (1822-86): a lieutenant in the Life Guards of the Calvary-Grenadiers. He took an active role in both the Petrashevsky and the Durov circles. At a luncheon held for members of the Durov circle at the home of Speshnev, he read his "Soldiers' Conversation," a work considered to be subversive for its criticism of administrative and military authorities. He was a member of the group of seven who wanted to establish a private printing press to disseminate articles promoting an upheaval in Russia. On the eve of his arrest, Dostoevsky had stopped by Grigoriev's and borrowed a banned book, Eugene Sue's *Berger de Kravan*. Grigoriev was sentenced to be shot but his sentence was commuted to fifteen years of penal servitude. As a result of his incarceration, the mock execution and penal servitude, he suffered from mental derangement from which he never recovered.

Kaidanov, Vladimir Ivanovich (1821-85): a friend of Petrashevsky from school days, employed as a civil servant. He was arrested and then freed and placed under surveillance.

Kashevsky, Nikolai Adamovich (1820-?): a civil servant in the Naval Ministry. He attended both Petrashevsky's and Durov's gatherings, playing music at the latter. According to Dostoevsky, he was more interested in his music than in the discussion which took place in the Durov circle. He was not tried.

Kashkin (mistakenly referred to in the testimony as Kashin), Nikolai Sergeevich (1829-41): a civil servant in the Asiatic Department of the Ministry of Foreign Affairs. Dostoevsky denies having been acquainted with him, although this does not appear to have been the case. For his participation in the Petrashevsky group he was sentenced to labor for four years but this sentence was commuted to military service. Kashkin was the son of one of the Decembrists.

Kraevsky, Andrei Alexandrovich (1810-89): a journalist and the publisher of *Notes of the Fatherland,* which printed several of Dostoevsky's early works. In his testimony, Dostoevsky mentions Kraevsky as one of the few people he was in contact with, not because this necessarily was the case but because Kraevsky would not arouse the suspicion of the Commission.

Kropotov, Dmitri Andreevich (1818-?): an orderly officer in the 1st Military School. He had been involved in the publication of the *Pocket Dictionary of Foreign Terms,* along with Petrashevsky and Valerian Maikov. Dubelt claimed that Kropotov was an agent of the Third Department, although nothing substantiates this claim. He was not tried but placed under secret surveillance.

Kuzmin, Pavel Alexandrovich (1819-85): staff-captain at General Headquarters. Kuzmin was a member of the Petrashevsky group who was not tried.

Lamansky, Evgeny Ivanovich (1824-1902) and Lamansky, Porfiry Ivanovich (1825-55): brothers employed in government service. They participated in both the Petrashevsky and Durov circles but were not tried.

Lvov, Fyodor Nikolaevich (1823-85): a staff-captain in the Life Guards of the Moscow Regiment who had been teaching chemistry in the Pavlovsky Military School. He participated in both the Petrashevsky and the Durov groups. His death sentence was commuted to twelve years of penal servitude.

Madersky, Alexander Timofeevich (1825-?): an auditor at Petersburg University and teacher. He lodged at Petrashevsky's where he attended the gatherings and, according to some testimony, helped to host them. He was not tried but was placed under secret surveillance.

Maikov, Apollon Nikolaevich (1821-97): a poet and long-time friend of Dostoevsky. Dostoevsky met him and his brother Valerian through Belinsky in 1846. Both Maikov brothers were acquainted with Petrashevsky and had attended his gatherings although not in the latter period. Nikolai Maikov turned down Dostoevsky's invitation for him to join the group involved with the printing press and he remained one of the few outsiders to know about this secret group and their plan. Maikov and Dostoevsky remained close friends, with Maikov serving as Dostoevsky's major tie to the Russian literary and intellectual scene during his long stay abroad in the late 1860s.

Maikov, Valerian Nikolaevich (1823-47): a literary critic who had been involved, along with Petrashevsky, in the publication of the *Pocket Dictionary of Foreign Terms*. Dostoevsky had known Valerian Maikov in the last year of his life and he remained close to the rest of the family thereafter. At the time of his death, Valerian Maikov had already become an important critic, taking a liberal viewpoint, but respectfully criticizing of Belinsky, whom he accused of lack of substantiation and a dictatorial stance. In his deposition, Dostoevsky appears to second this view when he terms Belinsky's letter a "model of lack of substantiation." The informer, Antonelli, mistakenly believed the two Maikov brothers, along with Dostoevsky, to be active in a literary group which had broken off from the Petrashevsky group.

Maikov, Nikolai Apollonovich (1794-1873): a painter and the father of Apollon and Valerian Maikov. Dostoevsky felt a fondness for the whole family and in a letter written to his brother prior to his exile he instructs his brother to send regards to Evgeniya Petrovna Maikova, the painter's wife.

Miliukov, Alexander Petrovich (1817-97): a literary historian, critic and journalist. Miliukov did not attend Petrashevsky's gatherings, although he was acquainted with many of those who did. He did participate in the Durov circle, where he read his translation of Lamennais's "Paroles d'un croyant." The Commission failed to focus attention on him. He was a friend and literary associate of Dostoevsky after his return from exile and was involved in the hiring of the stenographer, Anna Snitkina (who became Dostoevsky's second wife).

Mombelli, Nikolai Alexandrovich (1823-91): a lieutenant in the Life Guards of the Moscow Regiment. Mombelli had been actively involved in promoting an exchange of ideas among his fellow-officers in the military before he became associated with the Petrashevsky and Durov groups. The Investigatory Commission had been informed that he was one of the most dangerous members of the Petrashevsky group; the Commission focused its attention on a proposal he had made in the Durov circle for them to become more unified in an effort to propagate their views more effectively. He also participated in the secret conspiracy involving the printing press. He was sentenced to death; when the sentences were commuted he received fifteen years of hard labor, one of the most severe sentences.

Mordvinov, Nikolai Alexandrovich (1827-?): a civil servant in the Ministry of Internal Affairs who had graduated from Petersburg University. He participated in the Petrashevsky and Durov circles, as well as in the conspiracy involving the printing press, which was being kept in his home at the time of his arrest. According to Maikov's account, Mordvinov's family managed to keep the authorities from finding the printing press. Although arrested, Mordvinov was not tried; he was released but placed under surveillance.

Nabokov, Ivan Alexandrovich (1787-1852): the general in charge of the Peter-Paul Fortress where Dostoevsky and his co-defendants were incarcerated for the seven months of the investigation. He allowed others to carry out the interrogations, apparently because of his own incompetence in such matters.

Orlov, Alexei Fyodorovich: Chief Director of the Third Department of His Imperial Majesty's Own Chancellery and Chief of Gendarmes. Orlov played a major role in the decisions to watch, arrest and try members of the Petrashevsky group. He first assigned responsibility for the case to Liprandi and the Ministry of Internal Affairs when they brought it to his attention. Only later did he turn it over to Dubelt and the Third Department. He was in contact with the Tsar about the case.

Palm, Alexander Ivanovich (1822-85): a litterateur who shared an apartment with Durov. He participated in the Petrashevsky circle as well as in the circle meeting in his own home. He received a death sentence but was pardoned. He later wrote a novel, *Alexei Slobodin,* about the Petersburg circles of the late 1840s.

Petrashevsky (Butashevich-Petrashevsky), Mikhail Vasilievich (1821-66): a translator in the Department of Internal Relations of the Ministry of Foreign Affairs; he also held a law degree. He had contributed to the *Pocket Dictionary of Foreign Words*, a publication eventually banned, but which Petrashevsky had used to promote the socialist utopian ideas of Fourier, Saint-Simon and Owen. Petrashevsky began the gatherings at his home in 1845. While wholly committed to the liberal views aired in his house, Petrashevsky appears to have been more cautious than many of his visitors when it came to envisioning means for putting these views into practice. Dostoevsky in his testimony stresses the fact that no particular friendship existed between himself and Petrashevsky and this appears to have been the case. However, Petrashevsky told Antonelli (the police agent who infiltrated the group) that he was on very friendly terms with both Dostoevsky brothers. Petrashevsky was sentenced to death and when the sentences were commuted he received an open-ended sentence to penal servitude.

Pleshcheev, Alexei Nikoaevich (1825-93): a poet and litterateur. He was a close friend of Dostoevsky's. He was responsible for Dostoevsky's introduction to Petrashevsky and his group and he was also associated with members of the Durov circle. While staying in Moscow, he had sent Dostoevsky a copy of Belinsky's letter to Gogol. When Dostoevsky was arrested, a letter to him from Pleshcheev was found which contained some derogatory comments about the Tsar and court. He was sentenced to death, but this sentence was commuted to military service. A close affinity existed between Pleshcheev and Dostoevsky in the late 1840s, as is revealed in their respective works of the time. After Dostoevsky's exile, the two remained friends, despite their diverging politics.

Saltykov-Shchedrin, Mikhail Evgrafovich (1826-89): a writer and journalist who had attended Petrashevsky's gatherings. By the 1860s he had become a dominant figure in Russian letters of the time and *The Contemporary*, the liberal journal he and Nekrasov controlled, engaged in bitter polemics with the Dostoevsky brothers' journal.

Shchelkov, Alexei Dmitrievich (1825-?): a civil servant in the Chancellery of the Petersburg Military Governor-General. He lived with Durov and Palm and participated in their circle but was not tried.

Shmakov: a councillor of state in the Third Department. He was responsible for posing written questions to Dostoevsky for the latter's written response. He also composed the summaries of Dostoevsky's testimony, on the basis of which he was judged by the Military Court. These summaries are notable for their accurate, balanced representation of the material on which they are based.

Speshnev, Nikolai Alexandrovich (1821-82): a rich landowner who played a dominant role in the Petrashevsky and Durov circles, as well as in the plot to establish the printing press, which he is believed to have initiated and which he hoped would help bring about a political upheaval in Russia. For several years, he had lived abroad, where he had been involved with Polish patriots and had been exposed to communist ideology. He is generally accepted to have been the person most committed and suited to conspiracy among the various groups and is reported to have had strong personal influence on many of those involved, including Dostoevsky. Since the Investigatory Commission's file on him disappeared, his role remains somewhat mysterious. His death sentence was commuted to ten years of penal servitude.

Timkovsky, Konstantin Ivanovich (1814-81): a retired naval officer, employed in the Ministry of Internal Affairs. He lived in Tallin but would occasionally attend Petrashevsky's gatherings, where he gave an extended speech on Fourier which aroused the suspicion of the Investigatory Commission.

Toll, Felix Gustavovich (1823-87): a teacher of Russian literature in the Central Engineering Institute and of history at a military school. He figures in Dostoevsky's deposition simply because Dostoevsky had been asked about him in preliminary interrogation when the Commission was particularly alarmed about the Petrashevsky group's alleged intention to propagate Fourierism and other doctrines in educational institutions. Toll had also given a speech at Petrashevsky's about the origins of religion in which he promoted atheistic views. He also had a disagreement with Dostoevsky on esthetics. Toll was sentenced to death, but this sentence was commuted to penal servitude.

Yanovsky, Stepan Dmitrievich (1817-97): the doctor who treated Dostoevsky at the time. Yanovsky was also a close friend of Dostoevsky although he maintained conservative political views. Since he was in no way involved in the Petrashevsky circle, Dostoevsky could mention him in his testimony without fear of repercussions.

Yastrzhembsky, Ivan-Ferdinand Lvovich (1814-1880s): a teacher of political economy at the Technological Institute. He gave lectures on this subject at Petrashevsky's gatherings. Yastrzhembsky figures in Dostoevsky's deposition because he had been asked about him in the preliminary interrogation. Yastrzhembsky received a death sentence which was commuted to penal servitude, to which he was sent in the same convoy as Durov and Dostoevsky.

Zotov, Vladimir Rafailovich (1821-96): a journalist who edited *The Literary Gazette* from 1847 to 1849. He had been a classmate of Petrashevsky at the Lyceum.

II: Ideologies, Books and Documents

Belinsky's Correspondence with Gogol: This correspondence was initiated by Gogol who wrote to Belinsky to express his dissatisfaction with the latter's negative review of *Selected Passages from Correspondence with Friends*. In a response written on July 15, 1847, Belinsky sets forth his most sacred views on the vileness of the institution of serfdom, on the need for the elimination of corporal punishment, on the fact that those enforcing existing laws are criminals, on the obscurantism of the Church and the Russians' lack of religious sentiment. Belinsky felt that he and the Russian people had been betrayed by Gogol because the latter failed to use his position as a writer, a position which within the Russian context gave him great influence, to advocate social reform. Gogol had become, in Belinsky's words, "a preacher of the knout, an apostle of ignorance, a champion of obscurantism and barbarism, a panegyrist of Tatar ways." Since Gogol earned all these insults by championing the causes of autocracy and Russian Orthodoxy, Belinsky's criticism of Gogol is tantamount to an attack on these two mainstays of the regime and for these reasons the letter was considered criminal by the authorities.

Dostoevsky received a copy of this letter from Pleshcheev. At the time, copies of it were circulating in Moscow. The original appears to have been destroyed by Gogol and the existing copies are based on Belinsky's draft which he is said to have imparted to Granovsky just before dying.

The reading out loud of this letter at both Durov's and Petrashevsky's constituted Dostoevsky's major offense in the case.

Le Berger de Kravan: This was a book, officially banned in Russia, by Eugène Sue (1804-57), whose full title is: *Le Berger de Kravan: Entretiens socialistes et démocratiques sur la République et les prétendants monarchiques*. Sue's works show the influence of Fourier, Lamennais, Cabet, Saint Simon and Proudhon. However, Dostoevsky is known to have been attracted to them for their literary style, in particular for their suspenseful descriptions of the seamy side of city life. Dostoevsky had, according to this testimony, borrowed this particular book from Grigoriev only hours before his arrest and thus had not yet had a chance to read it.

Cabetism: This term designates the utopian socialism depicted by Etienne Cabet (1788-1856), particularly in his novel *Voyage en Icarie* (1840), an account of the voyage of an English lord to a fantastic country, Icarie, which is "ideally" governed according to the socialist principles. (Freedom of the press did not exist in Icarie and literature was strictly controlled by censorship.) Cabet believed that a period of dictatorship lasting fifty years was necessary to institute a socialist social system. He did not champion violent upheavals, maintaining that his system could be brought about peacefully by means of propaganda.

Although Dostoevsky mocks Cabetism in his deposition, this teaching was popular in Russia in the 'forties with, among others, Belinsky. (Writing years later in his *Diary of a Writer*, Dostoevsky lists Cabet along with George Sand, Pierre Leroux and Proudhon, as socialists that, according to Belinsky, Christ would have joined had he appeared on earth in the nineteenth century [*Diary of a Writer*, 1873, "Old People."])

La Célébration du dimanche: This book, whose full title is *De la célébration du dimanche considérée sous les rapports de l'hygiène publique, de la morale, des relations de famille et de cité* (1839), was officially banned in Russia. It is an early work of Pierre Joseph Proudhon (1809-65) in which this avowed "anti-theist" attacked industrial civilization and also indirectly criticized the Gospels.

Dostoevsky testifies that he borrowed this book from Golovinsky (without even asking permission) and that he had only read a few pages.

The influence of Proudhon, in general, was considered by the Investigatory Commission to be quite subversive. They had been informed of the fact that speakers at Petrashevsky's often referred to the theories of this socialist.

Fourierism: This term refers to the teachings of François Charles Marie Fourier (1772-1837), the utopian socialist who dreamed of organizing mankind into harmonious collectives inhabiting carefully designed "phalansteries." Fourierism aimed at developing human nature fully and freely by replacing individualism with cooperation and by taking advantage of innate human tendencies. (For example, the task of collecting garbage in the phalansteries was to be assigned to children since they, according to Fourier, feel no repugnance for the task and, on the contrary, enjoy it.)

Fourierism enjoyed great popularity among Russian intellectuals in the 1840s, evoking enthusiasm that in the previous decade had been associated with the teachings of Saint-Simon. Since Petrashevsky himself was a known "Fourierist," having attempted to preach these views in the *Dictionary of Foreign Terms,* and since many of his visitors shared his convictions, the Investigatory Commission focused great attention on this ideology.

In his deposition, Dostoevsky takes a somewhat condescending view of Fourierism, depicting its champions as ridiculous, impractical dreamers. In this fashion he attempts to minimize the threat of Fourierism in the eyes of the Investigatory Commission; however other evidence suggests that the view of Fourierism presented in the deposition was close to the one Dostoevsky actually adhered to at the time.

Moscow and Petersburg: This work, mistakenly referred to in the testimony as "Petersburg and Moscow," was written by Alexander Herzen and belongs to the series of feuilletons by various Russian writers, addressing the historical significance of Russia's two major cities. Herzen associates Petersburg with the autocracy and also refers to it as a "Babylon" and a city with neither history nor a future. He regards the city as a necessary evil in Russian life. While an expurgated version of this feuilleton had been published, the uncensored version read at Pleshcheev's contained satire and criticism considered subversive by the authorities.

Dostoevsky himself appears to have been familiar with this piece even before hearing it read at Pleshcheev's since he is thought to have been polemicizing with Herzen, among others, in his "Petersburg Feuilletons" written in the spring of 1847.

Paroles d'un croyant: This was an influential work by Félicité-Robert Lamennais (1792-1854), a cleric who turned to liberal political ideas and was considered to be something of a socialist revolutionary in the France of his day. Lamennais uses the style and form of biblical psalms and parables to illustrate how the political, economic and social reality contradicts religious values. He advocates human rights and political freedom.

To capture the biblical diction for a Russian-speaking audience, Miliukov translated this work into Church Slavonic. He read his translation at Durov's. In his testimony, Dostoevsky attempts to deflect the Commission's attention from the ideological content of the work by claiming the group to have been primarily interested in Miliukov's feat as translator. (And indeed for Dostoevsky himself, this was at least partially the case, for Miliukov reports in his memoirs that Dostoevsky praised his translation, saying that "the stern biblical language became more expressive in the translation than in the original.")

Petersburg and Moscow: See Moscow and Petersburg.

Soldiers' Conversation: This work, which Dostoevsky once refers to as "Soldiers' Tale," was written by Nikolai Grigoriev, a participant in both the Petrashevsky and the Durov circles. It consists of a conversation between soldiers which reveals their plight and in the process criticizes the military establishment, the government and the Tsar. Socialist ideas also figure. A copy of this work, which Grigoriev read to the Durov group during a gathering at Speshnev's, was found among Speshnev's papers.

NOTES

1. Dostoevsky's statements here and elsewhere, which aim at depicting Petrashevsky as an armchair Fourierist and nothing more, may not be entirely accurate since Petrashevsky is reported to have actually built a phalanstery on his estate (only to have it burned by the bewildered serfs who were supposed to populate it). However, the veracity of this story has been questioned by some scholars.

2. Within the Russian context at the time, the term "freethinking" was applied to any liberal tendency that challenged or criticized Russian Orthodoxy and autocracy, but it was particularly associated with the influence of Western European liberal ideology, such as that of Proudhon.

3. Some have suggested that Dostoevsky's talk on "individuality and human egoism" might have been a response to Max Shtirner's *Der Einzige und sein Eigentum* (1844).

4. In this passage of his deposition, Dostoevsky treats a theme which figures prominently in his literary works of the period, that of the lack of acceptable outlets for the individual's civic concern. Since the social structure denies citizens any opportunity to participate in politics and social issues, frustrated, they must find alternatives, the principal one being the formation of the so-called "circles" (kruzhki)— groups of individuals drawn together by a common interest. While participation in these circles was, in Dostoevsky's view, preferable to isolation, it failed to satisfy the individual's desire for fruitful activity since it consisted largely of talk, or more accurately, of petty argument.

5. Dostoevsky here discusses the revolutionary upheavals occurring in Western Europe in 1848, which he and the other members of the Petrashevsky group had been anxiously following from afar. The crackdown on the Petrashevsky group can partly be seen as the regime's attempt to insure that the revolutionary spirit not be enacted in Russia. Repressive measures in effect since the Decembrist revolt in 1825 had already made any liberal political activity next to impossible.

6. The possible influence of the French historian Augustin Thierry has been found in Dostoevsky's interpretation of the 1848 upheavals as a historical necessity and as a predetermined clash between the native populace and the authority which had artificially imposed itself on it.

7. In his assertion that Russia's historical destiny differs dramatically from that of the turbulent West (an assertion no doubt intended to appease the Investigatory Commission), Dostoevsky gives a foretaste of his political views of the 1860s.

8. In 1848 the tsarist regime had indeed strengthened its control on literature by instituting even more repressive censorship.

9. Alexander Griboedov (1795-1829) and Denis Fonvizin (1745-92) were major Russian playwrights known for their social satire. Alexander Pushkin (1799-1837) wrote poetry, prose and drama and, since he was at that time the best-known and best-loved Russian author, often termed the "father of Russian literature," the assertion that under the present censorship Pushkin could not exist was meant to be ultimate proof of the threat the censorship posed to literature.

10. Mikhail Lomonosov (1711-65) was a scientist, poet and philologist, and a key figure in Russia's newly founded Academy of Sciences. Dostoevsky here has in mind Lomonosov's role in instituting linguistic reforms aimed at standardizing literary Russian and thus making possible the emergence of Russian literature—Lomonosov's own poetry included.

11. Vissarion Belinsky (1810-48), the liberal critic who was ideologically one of the most influential literary figures of his time, befriended Dostoevsky upon reading the manuscript of *Poor Folk*. Relations between the two men deteriorated when Belinsky was disappointed by Dostoevsky's subsequent works, which failed, in his view, to treat pressing social issues.

Dostoevsky is also said to have been alienated from Belinsky because of the latter's lack of sympathy toward religion.

12. Ivan Krylov (1769-1844) was a major Russian fabulist, known for his ear for Russian. The morals of his fables are of a down-to-earth, conservative nature. Dostoevsky defended Krylov against Petrashevsky's attempts to disparage his importance as a writer able to appeal to the masses.

13. In Dostoevsky's preliminary interrogation and in the early stages of the investigation in general, the Commission was especially concerned with the fear that members of the Petrashevsky group had been attempting on a large scale to corrupt youth by converting them to Fourierism. As the investigation proceeded, the Commission concentrated on the propagation of subversive ideas and literature which took place within the confines of the Petrashevsky and Durov groups.

14. Petrashevsky was known for his personal library. The books it contained, which Dostoevsky here terms "rare," were often ones considered subversive by the tsarist regime. His visitors enjoyed the privilege of reading these books. Dostoevsky was criticized by some members of the Petrashevsky group for his lack of hard knowledge of Fourier and other promoters of new social theory. However, it has been established that Dostoevsky did take advantage of Petrashevsky's library to some degree, having borrowed the following books: Jean Joseph Blanc's *Histoire de dix ans, 1830-1840;* Etienne Cabet's *Le Vrai Christianisme suivant Jesus Christ*, Gustave Beaumont's *Marie; ou, L'Esclavage aux Etats-Unis*; Amédée Paget's *Introduction à l'étude de la science sociale contenant un abrégé de la théorie sociétaire, précédé d'un coup d'oeil général sur l'état de la science sociale, et sur les systèmes de Fourier, d'Owen et de Saint-Simon.* (The fact that he borrowed these books does not, of course, guarantee that he read them.)

15. Revel was the name then used for Tallinn, the major city of Estonia. Dostoevsky went there to visit his brother, Mikhail, on May 24, 1846.

16. The "estate" which would be requesting judicial reform from the government, according to Petrashevsky, is not identified but it would seem that the gentry (*dvorianstvo*) is meant. Petrashevsky clearly believed in the political responsibility of the privileged estate, the gentry, to instigate reform.

17. In 1861 the government finally emancipated the serfs, granting them land for which they were required to reimburse the landlords on an installment plan. However, these "Redemption Payments" turned out to be impossibly steep and were cut and eventually cancelled.

18. Other evidence supports this assertion that the members of the Durov group had hoped to publish a literary anthology, although nothing ever came of this particular plan and the energies of several in the group were diverted to their secret conspiracy to print material aimed at promoting a political upheaval in Russia.

19. Dostoevsky spent the summer of 1848 in Pargolovo.

20. The word "social" has been used to translate the Russian *sotsial'nyi* here and elsewhere in the testimony. In the context of the 1840s, the Russian term was closely associated with socialism. As the Investigatory Commission's question suggests, a "social" orientation was tantamount to a "liberal" one. Both were considered "freethinking."

21. Chernosvitov's alleged remarks further attest the identification between socialism and liberalism discussed in the note above.

22. Speshnev was quoting the proverbial expression about a "pal'ka o dvukh kontsakh" (a stick with two ends) used in reference to something which "cuts both ways."

23. These questions about Valerian Maikov appear to have been prompted by the misinformation received from Antonelli about a faction of the Petrashevsky group which consisted of litterateurs and was headed by the Maikov and Dostoevsky brothers.

24. The information conveyed by Antonelli had contained errors, such as the claim that Dostoevsky attended Petrashevsky's on March 11th, 18th and 25th. After Dostoevsky testified that he had been home sick during the month of March, these dates were crossed out in pencil.

25. The translation of Lamennais was actually read by Miliukov rather than Filippov.

26. Filippov, rather than Mombelli, was given Belinsky's letter to copy. (This mistake is repeated below.)

27. The term "unemployed nobleman" has been used to translate *nesluzhashchii dvorianin* which technically refers to a member of the nobility who has never served in the military or civil service and thus has no official rank.

28. A "candidate" (*kandidat*) .was the rank bestowed on someone who had finished the University; it was the equivalent of a lieutenant in the military or of a collegial secretary in the civil service.

29. The Russian term *meshchanin* was the official designation of members of the urban lower middle class. (Unlike the majority of his co-defendants, Shaposhnikov was not a member of the estate of nobles.)

30. The High Military Court added to Dostoevsky's offenses the intention to lithograph subversive materials (which the Military-Judicial Commission had not mentioned in its sentence). The court had in mind the discussion about lithography which took place at Durov's. The court was unaware that Dostoevsky had actually ben involved in the acquisition of the printing press, an offense which Speshnev and Filippov admitted to.

31. The Tsar showed mercy to Dostoevsky. Not only did he shorten the sentence, but he also effectively returned to Dostoevsky his civil rights (which someone sentenced to penal servitude normally lost forever) by making him a private in the army after four years of penal servitude. According to Miller, Dostoevsky assigned great significance to the fact that the Tsar intervened for him in this way. (The Tsar did however order some of the other sentences reduced in a similar fashion.) (See: Miller, pp. 114-15.)

32. Dostoevsky is reported by Miller to have taken the presence of the priest as a sign that the execution was going to be carried out. (Dostoevsky assumed that a priest would not have been made to participate in a hoax.)

On the other hand, another of the defendants, Kashkin, began to suspect that something was amiss when he happened to notice that the priest, who was there to confess the defendants, did not have the holy sacraments with him, whereas ordinarily after confession communion was administered. Kashkin managed to ask one of the officers standing near him about this and learned that they would all be pardoned. Apparently, he was the only one of the defendants who knew that the execution would not actually take place. (Miller, pp. 118-19).

33. The breaking of swords symbolized the loss of civil rights; it was a ritual undergone by criminals about to be executed as well as by those being sentenced to penal servitude. (Palm was spared this ritual because, at the recommendation of the General-Auditoriat, which the Tsar approved, he had been pardoned and was to be transferred into the army.)

34. St. George's Day was associated with unexpected bad luck and this phrase was a fixed expression used any day of the year to greet an unexpected turn-of-events for the worse; by coincidence, the Petrashevsky's group's arrest had coincided with the actual St. George's Day, April 23rd.

35. Leonty Vasilevich are the first name and patronymic of General Dubelt.

36. Dostoevsky probably paid his visit to Maikov in 1849 rather than 1848.